Look Around

Look Around

A Christian Faith for the Twenty-First Century

GEORGE R. SINCLAIR JR.

WIPF & STOCK · Eugene, Oregon

LOOK AROUND
A Christian Faith for the Twenty-First Century

Copyright © 2020 George R. Sinclair Jr. All rights reserved. Except for brief quotations in critical publications or reviews, no part of this book may be reproduced in any manner without prior written permission from the publisher. Write: Permissions, Wipf and Stock Publishers, 199 W. 8th Ave., Suite 3, Eugene, OR 97401.

Wipf & Stock
An Imprint of Wipf and Stock Publishers
199 W. 8th Ave., Suite 3
Eugene, OR 97401

www.wipfandstock.com

PAPERBACK ISBN: 978-1-7252-6668-1
HARDCOVER ISBN: 978-1-7252-6669-8
EBOOK ISBN: 978-1-7252-6670-4

Manufactured in the U.S.A.   06/16/20

To the future of my grandchildren,
Callum, Patrick, Eleanor, Ricky, Declan, and Cora

Contents

Acknowledgments		ix
Introduction		xi
Chapter 1	Who Is God?	1
Chapter 2	Who Am I?	9
Chapter 3	What Is Faith?	15
Chapter 4	What Is Grace?	22
Chapter 5	What Is The Bible?	29
Chapter 6	Creation or Evolution?	36
Chapter 7	Why Did Jesus Die?	43
Chapter 8	Why Was Jesus Raised From The Dead?	50
Chapter 9	What Does God Want From Us?	57
Chapter 10	A Chosen Few Or A Multitude Of Nations?	63
Chapter 11	Why Suffering?	70
Chapter 12	Is There No Justice?	78
Chapter 13	Who Is My Neighbor?	88
Chapter 14	What Is Prayer?	95
Chapter 15	Why Church?	104
Chapter 16	Why Worship?	114
Chapter 17	Why Work?	122
Chapter 18	God Before Country?	132
Chapter 19	How Do I Know God's Will?	142
Chapter 20	World Without End?	150
Chapter 21	Where Are You?	160
Bibliography		169

Acknowledgments

This book grew out of an impromptu conversation with my daughter. Thank you Meredith for giving me the nudge I needed. Throughout this project I benefited from the scholarship of three colleagues. I am deeply grateful to The Rev. Drs. Curtis Fussell, Al Reese Jr., and C. D. Weaver for their time, insights, and friendship. A number of lay readers offered generous support. Among those who read the entire work are Ann Adams, Kate Carver, Thomas Gore, MD, and Mark Johnson. Their honesty and perspective kept my feet on the ground. Dr. John Mulder, past-president of Louisville Presbyterian Theological Seminary, and Dr. Bill Brown, Professor of Old Testament at Columbia Theological Seminary, encouraged me to publish and provided helpful guidance. The staff of Wipf & Stock made production a pleasure. This book reflects the living hope of four congregations in Illinois, North Carolina, Georgia, and Alabama, where I witnessed faith and faithfulness over the course of forty years of parish ministry. It also reflects the lived faith of my parents and extended family. My sisters, Sandra, Stephanie, and Sylvia, have been patient listeners and great encouragers. My son, Sean, as always, inspires me with his perseverance and determined hope. My wife deserves the biggest thanks for enduring my absences, crankiness, and preoccupation. Paula's attention to detail and willingness to read and critique multiple drafts made this work far better. Our life together remains a source of wisdom and joy.

Introduction

Go up to the top of Pisgah and look around. —Deut 3:27

I have never visited Mount Pisgah, located east of the Jordan River and north of the Dead Sea, but I have hiked portions of the North American national forest by the same name. Moses hiked to the top of his summit because God sent him there for a panoramic view of the promised land. My expedition came under the direction of a Boy Scout leader in a remote area of the Pisgah National Forest named Wiseman's View, an escarpment on the western edge of Linville Gorge crossed by the Appalachian Trail.

To reach Wiseman's View, drive north on US 221 out of Marion, North Carolina (population 7,640). Marion is about thirty-six miles east of Asheville, North Carolina. When you reach the community of Linville Falls (population 140), hang a right onto NC 183 for one mile and then turn right at the big sign, *Linville Gorge*, onto old NC 105. Be careful; the graveled, potholed, and rutted road is not intended for faint-hearted suspensions, but when you reach your destination four miles later the vista will take your breath away.

Named for a Londoner in the 1700s, Wiseman's View looks over Linville Gorge (the *Grand Canyon of the East*), formed by the Linville River. For perspective, if the first floor of the One World Trade Center was street level at the river's bed and you were standing on Wiseman's View, you would have to look down to see the tower's 1254th floor and its bird's eye observation deck.

Wiseman's View is located near the center of the 500,000-acre Pisgah National Forest. Four hundred and eighty million years ago Wiseman's View was nestled in the navel of Pangea—the Appalachian Mountains. The Appalachians today stretch fifteen hundred miles from the island of Newfoundland southwestward to central Alabama. Back in the day when the world was literally one, the Ordovician predecessor of Wiseman's View was not far from geological remnants which today extend from Morocco in North Africa to Scotland's highlands. In those really old days, Wiseman's View was on top of the world, at least as high as the Alps and maybe even the Rockies, though not the Himalayas. Then again, in those days, these younger three were not yet formed, so maybe Wiseman's was on top after all.

With an elevation of just over five thousand feet, Wiseman's may not be as vertiginous as those titans ancient or modern, but it sure wobbled my knees. There was no railing and when I drew near to the edge looking east across the gorge to Hawk's Bill and Table Rock Mountain(s), it felt as if magnetism pulled me while a voice inside whispered, *You could fall or jump, George, and where would you be?* I approached with trepidation—crawling on my knees. Gazing across the expanse I tried taking in blue peaks and valleys of mile upon mile of old growth forest caressed by meandering white and still water whose roar could be heard when the wind was just right. Being perched on that edge was at once terrifying and inspiring. A confluence of fear and beauty arrested me in awesome wonder.

Fifty years later I am flooded by a similar confluence when I look around. I see rocks below. Chaos swirls around the human family: uncertainties in governments and financial markets; gun violence in schools and public spaces; opioid and other massive addictions; institutional erosion and collapse ranging from public libraries and PTAs to universities and hospitals, from once spired and inspirational churches to virtual social networks where friends no longer actually embrace; political allegiances defined by *Red States* and *Blue States*; climate change driven disasters, lost biodiversity and species extinctions; information overload coupled with underwhelming wisdom; xenophobia fueled by mass migrations; cultural wars, overpopulation, resource depletion, and a growing gap between the haves and have nots.

I also see promise: from medical advances and increasing health care access to prodigious food production capacity and colossal distribution networks; growing awareness of resource depletion and greater use of renewable energy alternatives; less despotism and more democracy; worldwide reduction in deaths by violence; less superstition and more scientific knowledge available to millions through multiple platforms; wider recognition of the one world we inhabit and robust collaboration among nations to care for the earth we all share. What would you add to these lists? What do you see when you look around? Where does it lead, to what end? And what does it mean? Is there some purpose to it all? And if so, where do you fit in?

This look around is written from the edge. In one way or another we all walk there. I am convinced it has always been that way. Humans have always found faith there—on the edge. Imagine Moses on Pisgah wondering about a land he could see but would never enter. Faith lives on the edge. It is born and thrives between peril and promise, certainty and uncertainty, enchantment and disenchantment, life and death. We can't and don't have one without the other. We live "through faith for faith" (Rom 1:17). When we look around "through faith for faith" we may discover God in the middle of everything that we find beautiful and terrifying. We may find God at work making all things new.

This book invites readers to look around and imagine the world differently. It is written for people of faith, for those of uncertain faith, and those of no expressed faith. I will refer to widely used theological terms and historic debates, but other works should be consulted for comprehensive reviews. While chapters are ordered sequentially, readers may prefer to read them topically.

This is not the thirteen century BCE when Moses climbed Pisgah or the first century when Jesus was led up the hill beyond Jerusalem's gates. This is not the age of Augustine or Aquinas or Luther or Calvin or that of their seventeenth and eighteenth-century heirs. This is the epoch of the Anthropocene begun by the fossil fuels revolution, accelerated by nuclear weaponry, now wrapped in a worldwide web.

Geologists reference Earth's 4.5 billion-year existence using five time signatures: eons, eras, periods, epochs, and ages. For a comparative scale consider years, months, days, hours, and seconds. Anthropocene is a relatively new designation. For many years Holocene was the designation for the epoch since the last Ice Age twelve thousand years ago until now. Beginning in the 1970s Anthropocene was used informally among scientists to express the consequences of human impacts on Earth's geology and ecosystems. Though not settled science, Anthropocene, which combines two Greek words meaning *human* and *recent*, captures not only human impacts on the environment but also a prevailing ethos of our time. Words like *secular* or *disenchanted* are frequently used to describe that ethos. While helpful and while used in this book, they do not adequately express the dislocation of God and radical elevation of the human over the last two hundred years.

We live in a thoroughly anthropocentric epoch. This book anticipates a Christian faith for this hour by inviting you to consider modest answers to questions humans have always faced but now face in a world where humans are viewed as the apogee of creation. This book is an invitation to take another look and imagine our world theocentrically which creates flourishing for humans while caring for God's creation.

Might a world theocentrically imagined relocate us as stewards rather than owners of Earth? Might a world theocentrically imagined recognize the impossibility of unlimited growth while managing to live in a world of limited resources? Might a world theocentrically imagined fund daily wants and needs but not at the expense of tomorrow? Might a world theocentrically imagined champion cooperation rather than competition, symbiosis rather than exploitation, integration rather than isolation? Might a world theocentrically imagined encourage mutuality rather than independence, interdependence rather than dominion, sustainability rather than consumption?

To see the world theocentrically acknowledges that the apogee of creation is not the sixth day when humankind was created, but the seventh day when God rested. A world theocentrically imagined relocates humankind. We are not masters or owners. We are guests, stewards, and sojourners invited to enjoy the beauty and goodness of creation blessed and hallowed by the Creator.

Through these essays I hope to engage you in a work of theocentric imagination. We do not get to choose the world we have but we do choose how we live in it. I hope this book encourages you to live more completely "through faith for faith" as you look around and discover the Creator who redeems and the Redeemer who creates in the fellowship of the Spirit who delights in the beauty of love.

Chapter 1

Who Is God?

BEGINNINGS

In the beginning when God created . . . —Gen 1:1

The human capacity for wonder is ancient and profound. Between 100,000 and 250,000 years ago our ancestors began to speak.[1] Approximately 70,000 years ago something like a "cognitive revolution" occurred—a capacity to imagine the unseen emerged, an ability revealed by cave art and burial remnants.[2] With the end of the last Ice Age, the capacity to experience and think about the unseen reached new dimensions with the advent of agriculture and the beginnings of civilization. Another eight thousand years would pass before stories appeared about the God spoken of in the Bible.

The story of this God begins when a wanderer named Abram left the city of Uruk around four thousand years ago. By the time of Abram, the Sumerian city was already fifteen hundred years old. Nine hundred years before Abram migrated from the land between the Tigris and Euphrates to the land of Canaan, the walled city of fifty to eighty thousand was the world's largest. The greatest monument within Uruk was the Anu Ziggurat topped by the White Temple dedicated to the sky god Anu. Construction of portions of the site required as many as fifteen hundred laborers, each working ten hours daily for five years. Work was not volunteered or compensated.

---

1. Bellah, *Religion in Human Evolution*, xviii.
2. Harari, *Sapiens*, 3.

The temple served a dual purpose—Sumerian kings and court officials were representatives of Anu. Honoring the king and court honored the god. The temple maintained a hierarchical social order keeping those on top in charge and those below in place. How God is imagined is not without consequence.

Nearly a thousand years elapsed between the time of Abram and the first stories written about him. The text cited from Genesis was written nearly 1,400 years later, sometime after the collapse of the kingdom of Judea in 587 BCE. The priests of Israel who gave us Abram's story, framed by the creation story, did not invent the idea of God. While they borrowed from surrounding cultures, they also recast their notions about God in ways radically different from neighboring cultures. The history of the idea of God is beyond the scope of this book. My primary interest is to invite reflection by asking you to consider some of the ways we use the word *God* today. Our use of the word, like biblical antecedents, is closely tied to culture. The phrase *In God We Trust*, for example, was added to United States currency in 1956. Did Congress have in mind the God of Abram and Moses who gave strict orders forbidding graven images; or equally ironic, was Congress thinking about Jesus who taught that humans cannot serve God and money?

When tweens today use the word *God* to accent sarcastic sighs and gleeful exclamations or when adults bless and curse by invoking God, what God is imagined? When serious scholars attach the word *God* to the titles of thick books, which God is their referent? When presidents bless nations in God's name and when players point to the sky, what God is invoked—a God who blesses the mighty, a God who favors winners? Our times are routinely labeled secular or disenchanted or anthropocentric, but the word *God* appears everywhere—but exactly which God or whose God? And what is this God like?

Is the God invoked by government a God who condones violence or one who commends peace? Does the God pointed to in the sky only applaud winners? What about losers? What about the small? Does God care if hungry children die? And if God cares, how is care displayed? What about good and evil? Does God keep score of right and wrong? Are some punished with eternal torments while others are awarded bliss? Is God merciful but not just or just but not merciful? Is God loving but not powerful or powerful but not loving? Who is God? What is the meaning of this three-letter word?

All ideas are negotiated and contingent. All definitions, including our definitions of God are made by people. I realize this is stating the obvious, but it must be said. Ideas about God do not fall out of heaven. We create them. That does not make God a work of sheer imagination, but it does say out loud that you and I must take responsibility for how we talk about God. That might make us nervous (and perhaps some days it does), but it should also make us humble and vigilant. Even at our best and even when describing ordinary, everyday phenomena, definitions are never perfect, which means we should constantly revise, correct, extend, and sometimes toss altogether definitions of important, complex ideas. The most significant ideas we imagine refuse to be pared down, flattened, or reduced. How we talk about big ideas matters, including and most especially, the idea of God. Imagining God is alternately exhilarating and daunting. From time to time, it may also require rearranging previously settled notions which can have decided impacts on the future of creation and how we live.

Think about Copernicus. Before Copernicus humans imagined that the sun, moon, and stars revolved around the earth. Copernicus had another idea. He dislocated heaven and earth or more accurately relocated them. For millennia our forebears agreed that everything revolved around Earth. It appeared self-evident. Anyone who looked around could see that the sun rose in the east and set in the west. Copernicus had a different way of modeling heaven and earth. He started a revolution. So did Luther and Calvin, Jefferson and Adams, Smith and Marx, Darwin and Einstein, along with a host of others who had the gumption and imagination to ask: Have you ever wondered about . . . ?

How about God? How would you define God? For starters; how about the *omnia*? We commonly say God is all-powerful, all-knowing, all-present. How about prepositions? We say God is up, above, and over us; in, among, and with us. These position locators reference transcendence and imminence or more commonly heaven and earth. How about time references which direct us to concepts like immortal and eternal or descriptors like invisible and immutable? They seem to apply along with the often invoked term *super-natural* denoting that God is greater than or beyond nature. How about actions and works? What does God do? And what does God not do? What about character or disposition? What is God like? And what is God not like? Before taking a stab at some answers, I wish to pause.

Books, like soup cans, should identify ingredients. A label on a can I picked from my kitchen cabinet read: Tomato puree (water, tomato paste), high fructose corn syrup, wheat flour, water, contains less than 2 percent of: salt, potassium chloride, flavoring, citric acid, lower sodium natural sea salt, ascorbic acid (vitamin C), monopotassium phosphate. When you open a can of soup you ought to know what you are getting. Likewise, books should disclose writer identity. Here is mine: I am a Christian and a retired minister of the Presbyterian Church (U.S.A.).

As I speak about God I do not presume to speak for Jews or Muslims or other respected faith traditions. For that matter, I do not presume to speak for all Christians or even all Presbyterians. I do not say this with prejudice toward Muslims or Jews or people of other faith traditions. What I am saying is that while we may share a working definition of God, perhaps something like the super-natural deity sketched above, we also communicate from particular social locations. Mine happens to be Christian and Presbyterian, which means that my understanding of God is molded and modified by Scripture and a particular Christian tradition extending to John Calvin among many others. Like all Scripture readers I privilege some Bible texts over others. And like all readers the texts I privilege are brought into focus (or not) through the particular lens of my social location and tradition which extends beyond descriptors like Presbyterian and Christian to include others like white, male, retired, husband, father, grandfather, etc. With this brief but necessary disclosure, I return to the question: Who is God?

MYSTERY

I found among them an altar with the inscription, "To an unknown god." —Acts 17:23

The pioneers whose footprints are left in the Bible walked their broad and sometimes narrow path drawn by powerful mystery. They did not believe that God was a mere projection of imagination handy for meeting their needs and desires. To the contrary, they believed God disclosed his identity through his works and words. Many of these pioneers fiercely acknowledged that while God is disclosed, mystery is never fully resolved. The unresolvable character of mystery pulls us into its orbit which is at once orienting and disorienting. Mystery keeps us on the edge. Falling in love is like that. Who can explain attraction, not the everyday garden variety type but a once in a lifetime, walk across a thousand-mile-desert kind? Mystery creates tension. It enlivens us. Imagine life without it—we would be bored out of our minds. The mystery of God is something like that. Consider what two pioneers concluded.

The first is the prophet, Isaiah, who invited readers to overhear God more or less muttering to himself about us, "My thoughts are not your thoughts, nor are your ways my ways. . . . As the heavens are higher than the earth, so are my ways higher than your ways and my thoughts than your thoughts" (Isa 55:8–9). The second is the apostle, Paul, a contemporary of Jesus who raced over the entire Mediterranean persuaded and pursued by grace. In what was to become his last known letter, Paul strains to account for the peculiarities of faith and non-faith, concluding his effort with a shout of adoration, "O the depths of the riches and wisdom and knowledge of God!

How unsearchable are his judgments and how inscrutable his ways" (Rom 11:33). Like Isaiah, Paul proclaimed rather than explained the mystery of God. While doing so, neither pioneer sought refuge behind obscurity. Both painstakingly and publicly declared what they believed about God while arguing for the moral implications of their proclamation.

Isaiah and Paul remind us that God is greater than we imagine or can imagine. Humility is cautioned whenever we venture a word about God. Mystery, however, does not absolve us of deliberative thought or responsible action. Faith opens our eyes for witness in the public square.

DISCLOSURE

The grace of the Lord Jesus Christ, the love of God, and the communion of the Holy Spirit be with you. —2 Cor 13:13

How we talk about God matters, which is why Christians have wrestled with the mystery of God, settled disputes, and strived again to express who God is to the best of their understanding. Faith seeks understanding.[3] With the church universal I believe God is *One*—Father, Son, and Holy Spirit. Some will argue that the doctrine of the Trinity is not only a waste of time but simply wrong. It is true that the term does not appear anywhere in the Bible. And yes, not all versions of the Trinity are equally helpful. Some are not only fuzzy but plainly wrong. That said the idea of Trinity can help us avoid some not so happy or healthy or helpful conclusions about God. Let me repeat: what we believe about God has consequences. How we understand God has large implications for how we understand ourselves and live in our world.

My aim here is not to give a history of trinitarian thought but to outline a social doctrine of the Trinity, an idea expressed by the Greek word *perichoresis*, a compound of *peri* (around) and *choresis* (dancing). The idea of God *dancing around* was first used by Gregory of Nazianzus (fourth century) and brought into wider currency by the seventh-century Syrian theologian, John of Damascus. To explore this compelling though ancient way of thinking about God, I want to make a quick detour by way of neuroscience.

Paul MacLean was the third of four sons of a Presbyterian minister. After graduating from Yale, Edinburgh, and Harvard, MacLean joined the National Institutes of Health where he headed a new department on the limbic system in neurophysiology, which made great sense because MacLean was the first to name the limbic region of the brain. From 1971 to 1985 MacLean was chief of the NIH lab on brain evolution and behavior. In 1990 MacLean

---

3. Migliore, *Faith Seeking Understanding*, 2–5.

published a book titled *The Triune Brain in Evolution*. MacLean argued that the brain has three regions—the *limbic* which manages emotions, the *neocortex* which handles intellectual tasks, and the *reptilian complex* which generates self-preservation or more commonly our fight or flight response. MacLean tied these regions of the brain to evolution. He thought the oldest and most primitive was the *reptilian complex* or the lizard.

While MacLean separated brain regions by function he also integrated them, though not as closely as neuroscience does today. Likewise, it turns out that human brain development is far less linear than MacLean thought and far more punctuated. Hold both thoughts as we think about the Trinity.

Gregory and John did not imagine one God with three functions—the Father creates, the Son reconciles, and Holy Spirit redeems. Nor did they imagine creation, reconciliation, and redemption as successive, disparate works. These early Christian thinkers imagined God akin to the way more recent neuroscience maps the human brain. Their thinking about God was non-linear and integrated. In a like manner our imagining of God is helped by parting company with chronological, hierarchal, and compartmentalized thinking.

As a wise teacher observed, "all of God is involved in everything God does."[4] Or, as Jürgen Moltmann suggests, trinitarian thinking is helped when we abandon circles and triangles and think instead of kaleidoscopes and whirlwinds which, in his words, allows us to "conceive of a community without uniformity and a personhood without individualism."[5]

Thinking about God kaleidoscopically as a fellowship of the Father, Son, and Holy Spirit may help us avoid some binary traps. Here, in no particular order, are some common ones.

1. One God creates, commands, judges, and is generally angry and scary; while the other God, approachable and kind, befriends, redeems, and teaches with clever riddle and gentle irony.

2. One God rules with an iron fist; the other dies on a cross.

3. One God is invisible, immovable, impassive; the other visible, vulnerable, and compassionate.

4. One God resides eternally in heaven; the other was born in a barn.

5. One God sends, speaks, and rules; the other is sent, listens, and obeys.

6. One God chooses a tribe; the other elects all nations.

7. One God is remote; the other closer than the air we breathe.

---

4. Guthrie, *Christian Doctrine*, 85.

5. Moltmann, *Sun of Righteousness, Arise!*, 152–53.

Seven is a good number so I will stop. Binary thinking stifles understanding, which is not helpful when looking around for a twenty-first century faith. Monistic thinking is hardly better. Here are some examples.

1. God is all about love, but avoids justice.
2. God creates the earth, but we are on our own tending it.
3. God redeems humans, but leaves creation behind like a useless empty nest.
4. God dazzles the faithful with bliss, but blissfully ignores the faithless.
5. God is great with sunsets, but lousy with cancer.
6. God excels at commanding, but gives no help when law is insufficient to meet love's demands.
7. God is cool with poodles and rainbows, but hasn't the stomach for weapons of mass destruction and those who store them in concrete silos or move and hide them in deep seas.

If monistic and dualistic thinking falls short, how might we imagine God in trinitarian terms so that we avoid a cartoon Trinity who does not help and is likely a hindrance when looking around? To avoid caricatures like *The Enforcer, Buddy Jesus, and Jeeves*, it will help to remember that God is united yet distinct while distinguished but not separated in all of his works. A dynamic, integrated way of understanding God better navigates the path and enables us to look around with different eyes. Here are possible trajectories—again seven.

1. God creates through the Son to the delight of the Spirit.
2. Paraphrasing Faulkner, creation is never dead; it is not even past.
3. With a shout out to Calvin, creation is the theater of God's glory and not a disposable playground one day left behind.
4. The death of Jesus does not change the Father's disposition, but expresses it.
5. The Spirit is not an afterthought, remnant, or vestige of the Son, but is the Father stirring every breath for the good of everyone.
6. The Son suffers death for sinners, the Father suffers the Son's death, while the Spirit groans in travail birthing God's new creation.
7. The Father who is up, above, and over us is also the Son who is with and for us no less than the Spirit who is before, in, and among us.

God is greater than we imagine or can imagine. That is not an excuse for arrested curiosity or contentment with half-truth, but it may inspire us to walk lightly and yet with purpose on a path full of twists and turns and occasional dead ends. It may help us avoid creating idols which are projections of our desires. A trinitarian image of God faithfully rendered may guide our steps as we look around. The kaleidoscopic, social, dynamic Trinity outlined here is a modest beginning. The footsteps of this *dancing around* God who creates, reconciles, and redeems will mark subsequent chapters. The next turns to a second question of identity: Who am I?

Chapter 2

Who Am I?

GENES, GENEALOGY, AND GEOGRAPHY

You are dust and to dust you shall return. —Gen 3:19

You have made them a little lower than God. —Psalm 8:5

By the time you finish reading this sentence your body will have lost and replaced thousands upon thousands of the ten trillion cells that make you—you. In about nine years nearly all of the ten trillion cells that make you—you, will have been replaced, down to the very last molecule. That's a lot of molecules, some five million to two trillion in each and every cell. By then will you still be you? Or will you be a different you? Is identity stubbornly fixed, randomly fluid? or perhaps identity marches in fits and starts or flows through stages? What makes you—you? Who are you? When making new acquaintances we commonly reference our origins. Oh, I'm from North Carolina. My parents were from Wilmington. I was also born there but I grew up outside of Charlotte in a town called Gastonia; how about you? Beginnings are fascinating clues to identity so while making introductions let's take a closer look at genes, genealogy, and geography.

    Have you ever had your DNA tested? Ever been tempted to bite on one of those enticing gene-geography ads and send in a swab? I haven't done that . . . yet, but I did dig up a tattered letter typewritten by my father's brother which, together with my daughter's cyber-sleuthing, filled in some missing genealogical links.

In the mid-eighteenth century, my mother's ancestors sailed from England, coming ashore somewhere near or on Holden's Beach, North Carolina. Many never left the coast. Some, like my mother's father, made their way inland and settled in Wilmington, North Carolina, which is where the trail on the maternal side ends—or my search anyway. More links were available on the paternal branch of the family tree.

My father, the last of six siblings, was born in 1925 in Wilmington, North Carolina. His father, Roby Thomas Sinclair, an only child, was born in 1883. Roby's father, Francis Marion Sinclair, born during the Civil War in Moore County, North Carolina, was a rural route mail carrier in nearby Lee County before moving to Wilmington where he worked as a cobbler, a trade inspired by his club foot. Francis Marion's ancestors arrived in the port of Wilmington roughly one hundred years earlier on a ship named the *Ulysses* which had set sail from the west coast of Scotland in 1774. According to one record, Francis Marion's ancestors emigrated because of high rents and oppression, which sounds about right.

A more romantic telling of Clan Sinclair would lead to Castle Sinclair or what is left of it located on a rocky cliff overlooking a small bay and the North Sea three miles north of Wick, Scotland. The site, which dates from the fourteenth century, was likely chosen for its rugged terrain and daunting sea defenses which would have been handy when the Norse began arriving from Scandinavia in the late eighth century, or perhaps the Norse were the first to claim the barren outpost. The name *Wick* appears to be a Norse derivative meaning freebooter, sea rover, pirate or Viking; that is, one who comes from a fjord or *vik*, a creek, inlet, or small bay.

So my ancestors may have been Vikings! But then again, where did they come from? Between 9000 and 6000 BCE, Scandinavia was populated by semi-sedentary groups who left Afro-Eurasia around twelve thousand years ago at the end of the last Ice Age. Population pressure and competition drove peasants to leave milder climes to settle unforgiving lands they once likely scorned.[1] Again, that sounds about right.

My ancestors and yours, hungry and curious, have been on the move since migrating out of Africa seventy thousand years ago. We all come from somewhere and that somewhere is Africa. What does that mean? For starters it means we are wanderers. For another we are all related. By one estimate the most distantly related person on the planet is something like your seventy-eighth cousin.[2] Said otherwise, all people living today share the exact same ancestors who were alive in 2158 BCE, which means we are

---

1. Christian, *Origin Story*, 238.
2. Heine, *DNA is Not Destiny*, 144.

far more alike than different, genetically speaking anyway.[3] Our differences, which are considerable, are more a matter of geography than genes.

We are dust. We are of the earth, uniquely so—"a little lower than God." One famous origin story, dating from roughly three thousand years ago pressed together these divergent aspects of human identity this way: "[T]he LORD God formed man from the dust of the ground, and breathed into his nostrils the breath of life; and the man became a living being" (Gen 2:7). A later version conveys that we are made in the image of God (Gen 1:27).

We are dust and breath of life made in the image of God. Expressed in the Hebrew language of Genesis, we are *adamah* and *nephesh*. We are not one or the other but both together—all of us, every single one of us, all 7.7 billion and counting are made of earth and breath. We are royalty, every single one of us. That should give every one pause for ever thinking too highly or lowly of herself or of anyone else. Every life is worthy. No life is more worthy than any other life and no life is less worthy than any other life. Each and every human life is accorded royal status. And by virtue of this God-given standing each and every life is tasked with tending the garden which supports the dust and breath of life we are. Sometimes we are excellent tenders; sometimes we are absolutely dreadful. Though dust and breath created in the image of God we are distorted and warped and full of contradiction. We act contrary to the Creator's intention. That contrariness leaves us in a deep predicament, one we cannot escape except with help.

CONTRADICTIONS, DISTORTION, PREDICAMENT

I do not understand my own actions. —Rom 7:15

Which of the following have you said or heard or wanted to say: *She's not herself today. He never acts like that. I don't know what got into me. I don't know what came over me. Why did I do that? He must have been out of his mind. What was he thinking? Why is she acting that way? That's not like her. Look at me; over here. Can you see me? I've been waiting all day. Please notice me. Look my way. Oh, no. Don't look at me. Turn away. I'm a mess. Imagine if people could read my mind?*

"I don't understand my own actions." It is not an excuse; well, it may and can be, but it is more likely a statement of fact. We may be royalty but we are prone to make a royal mess. We are creatures of contradiction, divided against ourselves and often pitted against one another, even and sometimes especially against those we love most. Are we natured this way? Has nature

---

3. Heine, *DNA is Not Destiny*, 144.

selected altruism and cooperation as well as selfishness and competition to keep us alive?[4] Alternately, is there something called *sin* which creates a war within the dust and breath we are, a conflict between altruism and selfishness, a battle between competition and cooperation which invariably spills over to and against others who are no less conflicted?

Whether you imagine the fall as an event or a rhetorical device, and I think the latter, we humans are in a predicament. Even our best intentions have harmful unintended and unforeseen consequences. History professor and cofounder of the Big History Project, David Christian describes our predicament this way, "Can we preserve the best of the Good Anthropocene and avoid the dangers of the Bad Anthropocene? Can we distribute the Anthropocene bonanza of energy and resources more equitably to avoid catastrophic conflicts. . . . Or will we keep depending on flows of energy and resources so huge that they will eventually shake apart the fantastically complex societies we have built in the past two hundred years?"[5] The dust and breath of life we are malfunction, misfire, and routinely manage to compromise, foul, and destroy the otherwise life-giving space we inhabit. Like starlight bent by dark matter, we are pulled by proximate forces not of our making. The image of God which gives every single last one of us royal dignity and worth becomes distorted, twisted, warped, misshapen, and just plain crooked—despite and sometimes directly as a result of our best efforts. We are in a predicament, one that far surpasses our wisdom and power of extrication. We need large-scale intervention. We need help.

O GOD, I AM THINE

I come to the end—I am still with you. —Ps 139:18

On a gray Monday morning, April 9, 1945, Dietrich Bonhoeffer was summoned from his Flossenbürg cell by the Gestapo and ordered to disrobe. With five co-conspirators, the thirty-nine-year-old Lutheran pastor and theologian was led to the gallows and hung. His corpse, piled with others, was burned. Two weeks later, Allied Forces entered Flossenbürg. In three weeks Hitler was dead. It would be June before Bonhoeffer's twenty-year-old fiancée Maria von Wedemeyer learned of his death. His parents heard the news the following month. Ten years later the camp doctor of Flossenbürg recalled the morning of April 9.

---

4. Feinberg and Mallatt, *The Ancient Origins of Consciousness*, 219.
5. Christian, *Origin Story*, 282–83.

Through the half-open door in one room of the huts I saw Pastor Bonhoeffer, before taking off his prison garb, kneeling on the floor praying fervently to his God. . . . At the place of execution, he again said a short prayer and then climbed the steps to the gallows, brave and composed. His death ensued after a few seconds. In the almost fifty years that I worked as a doctor, I have hardly ever seen a man die so entirely submissive to the will of God.[6]

The prison doctor knew something about death. Thirty thousand people were killed by the Nazis at the Flossenbürg death factory. Despite this and other accounts, Bonhoeffer did not wish to be remembered as a hero or martyr. "The ultimate question for a responsible man to ask is not how he is to extricate himself heroically from the affair, but how the coming generation is to live. It is only from this question, with its responsibility towards history, that fruitful solutions can come, even if for the time being they are humiliating."[7] From Bonhoeffer's perspective our responsibility for history "depends on a God who demands responsible action in a bold venture of faith, and who promises forgiveness and consolation to the man who becomes a sinner in that venture."[8]

As attested by his prison letters, Bonhoeffer's journey to this stunning stance was not reached apart from homesickness, acedia, self-pity, plans for escape, and if briefly, thoughts of suicide. Few remnants reflect Bonhoeffer's extraordinary struggle more passionately than his poem titled "Who Am I?" Written in the summer of 1944, midway through an eighteen-month internment at Tegel, a German military interrogation prison in Berlin, Bonhoeffer wrote,

> Who am I? They often tell me I would step from my cell's confinement
> calmly, cheerfully, firmly,
> like a squire from his country house. . . .
>
> They also tell me I would bear the days of misfortune
> equably, smilingly, proudly,
> like one accustomed to win.
>
> Am I then all that which other men tell of?
> Or am I only what I know of myself,
> restless and longing and sick, like a bird in a cage,
> struggling for breath, as though hands were compressing my throat, . . .

---

6. Bethge, *Dietrich Bonhoeffer*, 830–31.
7. Bonhoeffer, *Letters & Papers from Prison*, 6.
8. Bonhoeffer, *Letters & Papers from Prison*, 7.

> weary and empty at praying, at thinking, at making
> faint, and ready to say farewell to it all?
>
> Who am I? This or the other?
> Am I one person today, and tomorrow another?
> Am I both at once? A hypocrite before others,
> and before myself a contemptibly woebegone weakling?
> Or is something within me still like a beaten army,
> fleeing in disorder from victory already achieved?
>
> Who am I? They mock me, these lonely questions of mine.
> Whoever I am, thou knowest, O God, I am thine.[9]

While the Flossenbürg physician witnessed a squire marching bravely to his end, composed and submissive to the will of God, Bonhoeffer saw a caged bird spent with prayer, a weakling, a hypocrite whose identity was shred and reshaped by the whirlwind of war. Which was the real Bonhoeffer? The young pastor, wise beyond his years, suspended a final answer, deferring instead to a judgment rendered by God, "Whoever I am, thou knowest, O God, I am thine."

Like the psalmist who fled from God only to learn that God was everywhere, Bonhoeffer concluded that in spite of the contradictions and distortions tormenting him and no matter the depth of his predicament, he belonged to God. Belonging meant freedom from the weary desire to prove himself in the court of public opinion or before the face in the mirror and most especially before God. Justification in those courts was not needed. Justification was given by God in Christ. Freed from the demand to prove himself Bonhoeffer was freed for responsible action in and on behalf of the world. He could tend the garden and represent God on Earth.

"I come to the end—I am still with you." The psalmist was not bragging. The conviction was no idle boast about personal steadfastness. To the contrary the psalmist testified to the wonder of God's extraordinary faithfulness and unwavering resolve. God abides—wherever we are—"even the darkness is not dark to you; the night is as bright as the day, for darkness is as light to you" (Ps 139:12). Looking around from the edge as we do, that is good news for the royally made dust and breath of life we are. In God's light we know who we are—shadows and all. In chapters that immediately follow we will explore how through *faith alone, grace alone,* and *Scripture alone* we are delivered from the shadows so that we may enjoy durable freedom to tend the garden and represent the One in whose image we are made.

---

9. Bonhoeffer, *Letters & Papers from Prison*, 347–48.

Chapter 3

What Is Faith?

FRIENDSHIP

Teacher, do you not care that we are perishing? —Mark 4:38

Is anything too wonderful for the LORD? —Gen 18:14

Is God both willing and able to intervene in the human predicament? And if God is able and willing, how do we know? We know by faith. And faith or the character of faith is shaped by the subject of faith, by the acts and character of God. Faith is a stance toward the world grounded in friendship created by the One who calls us to follow. Before saying more, let me state briefly what faith is not.

    First, and perhaps foremost, faith is not an effort to believe a long or short list of hard to believe things like: God made the world in seven days; God parted the Red Sea; Jonah was swallowed by a big fish; Jesus walked on water, was born of a virgin, turned water into wine, healed the sick, and was raised from the dead. Regardless of how we understand supernatural phenomena, (and my point is not to deny miracle, unfathomable outcomes, or the impossible becoming possible), faith should not be confused with gullibility, magical thinking, or a kind of silly optimism. Second, faith is not blind. Faith leans us into unknowns, but that should not be mistaken for ignorance. We would not call a chemist ignorant because she searched for a cancer cure, failed, and searched again. We would more likely call the researcher painstakingly persistent, if not heroic. Faith opens our eyes.

Faith leads to seeing, to understanding. While faith is not incompatible with reason, faith, as a consequence of its subject, is not discovered through reason. The *Subject* of faith, as the writer of Hebrews poetically observes, "is a consuming fire" (Heb 12:29). If people of faith are not gullible, blind, or irrational, what are they? To begin an answer let me tell a story.

Twenty-plus years ago I met a man I will call Captain A. J. When I first met A. J., I did not know he was a *captain*—he was a retired master mechanic for a major commercial airline who happened to like bicycles. A. J. and I rode together for years circling the red clay hills of west Georgia. You get to know a person well after spending two hours fighting headwinds in the blistering heat of summer. On those rides, I discovered many things about A. J., among them that he enjoyed sailing. He explained that he taught himself how to sail in Tokyo Bay in the 1950s when stationed at nearby Haneda Air Force Base. After returning to the states, A. J. learned celestial navigation before delivering the first of six sailboats from Hawaii to San Francisco. Though separated in age by seventeen years, A. J. and I became good friends.

On a ride one day A. J. asked if I would like to join him for a delivery leaving West Palm Beach bound for Newport, Rhode Island. The boat was a forty-two-foot *Little Harbor* sloop equipped with roller furling and reefing. We would be at sea for about seven days. All expenses paid, including air travel. I thought, *Why not? Sign me up.* I had never been on a sailboat, not even a *Sunfish*, but I loved the ocean and thought it would be an adventure. And so it was—all thirteen hundred miles on the open ocean. Just as we hit the ink-blue Gulf Stream we had great sailing weather—twenty knots on our nose which put the lee rail down and bow spray on the helm. What a ride. By nightfall the wind stopped, which is not ideal when you are 150 miles offshore, especially if a transmission breaks, which ours did. Not to worry, the next day the wind returned and the three of us on board agreed that we would make for New England. Aside from a not-so-kind squall, which resulted in another mate tossing his cookies, and several becalmed days, we had a great trip, including landing a delicious, twenty-pound Mahi Mahi. When I got off of the boat I could not walk straight but I had great stories to tell.

Getting on that boat had way more to do with Captain A. J. than it did me. I trusted him because he was trustworthy. I could not take a boat like that across a smooth lake much less a rolling ocean more than halfway up the East Coast. My sailing skills were nil. I barely knew a sheet from a halyard. I did my best to pull my weight, but there was never a doubt about who was in charge and that was perfectly okay by me, which is to say that faith is shaped and determined by what or who we trust. That is true whether we are talking about sailboat captains or the greatest wonder of all—God. Faith is created by the One we trust. Before all else faith is friendship with God.

STANCE

We are workers with you for your joy, because you stand firm in the faith. —2 Cor 1:24

On the night of my confirmation exam, a kindly leader of my church whose name I do not remember led me into the cavernous, empty sanctuary of my youth and showed me to a pew. Dressed in a dark suit and plain necktie, the elder took the pew in front of me. Turning around he smiled reassuringly and asked, "What is the chief end of man?"[1] Having rehearsed the concise answers with my parents, I straightened up and replied,

"Man's chief end is to glorify God, and enjoy him forever."

Nodding approval the elder continued, "What is God?"

"God is a Spirit," I said, "infinite, eternal in his being . . . ah . . . ?"

"Unchangeable . . . "[2] the elder prompted.

Mercifully the questions ended several halting answers later. The elder appeared relieved and proud. I must have passed the exam because the following Sunday night, along with a dozen or so other seventh graders, I was admitted into the faith. Among other recitals I displayed sufficient knowledge of the Apostles' Creed, Ten Commandments, and the Lord's Prayer.

While I did not memorize each of the one hundred-plus answers to *The Shorter Catechism*, the faith handed on to me by my church provided a framework for making sense of and living in the world. Had I memorized all one hundred answers I would not have been immune to other persuasive narratives competing for my adolescent attention and devotion: student, classmate, athlete, friend, and within a few short years—citizen and potential soldier. I had received a tradition. The greater question looming over my life was whether or not that tradition would become a living faith shaped and expressed by friendship with God.

TRUST

For by grace you have been saved through faith, and this is not your own doing; it is the gift of God. —Eph 2:8

1. Presbyterian Church (U.S.A.), *Book of Confessions*, 229.
2. Presbyterian Church (U.S.A.), *Book of Confessions*, 229.

How does faith become living friendship with God? Is friendship about obedience, sincerity, or some combination of the two? Can we be obedient but not sincere? Can we be sincere but not obedient? What are the signs of friendship with God?

John Calvin (1509-1564) defined faith as "a firm and certain knowledge of God's benevolence toward us, founded upon the truth of the freely given promise in Christ, both revealed to our minds and sealed upon our hearts though the Holy Spirit."[3] Calvin reasoned that faith is sufficient and not misplaced when it is located in God and not in us. The defining characteristic of God, according to Calvin, is "God's benevolence."[4] God's benevolence is not idle or earnest speculation. It is not wishful thinking or a projection of need fulfillment. God reveals his character in Christ and the *Character* revealed is the basis of our "firm and certain knowledge."

Faith does not create friendship with God. Faith does not generate conditions for trust. Our ability to stand firm, our capacity to trust God is grounded in God's benevolence disclosed in Christ which is "revealed to our minds and sealed upon our hearts through the Holy Spirit."[5]

Calvin's close reading of Scripture convinced him that faith is a gift. While faith involves cognition and emotion, and while faith is a human response, the accent does not fall on us. Whenever it does we are imperiled. That is the great tragedy of the Anthropocene Epoch—replacing faith in our Creator and Redeemer with faith in ourselves. The slide from a theocentric to anthropocentric faith is not obvious. Orthodoxy and Pietism suggest two ways that may occur.

Orthodoxy, with its accent on the mind, lays claim to right thinking, correct thinking—the form of faith. Pietism, anchored in the heart, whirls around intensity of feeling, depth of emotion, experience—the energy of faith. By way of analogy, the former is found in a classroom, the latter at a revival.

Cognition and emotion are not the sum of us. We possess aesthetic sensibilities and we have bodies, or we *are* body. Our response to God involves all that we are. When we are summoned to faith, we are prompted, stirred, and quickened in heart, soul, mind, body, and strength—but assurance that we have responded to God and not to a figment of our imagination resides with God.

My ardor did not take that sailboat to Rhode Island; and while I tried to follow orders and keep myself orderly, I was more or less along for the

---

3. Calvin, *Institutes*, 3.2.7.
4. Calvin, *Institutes*, 3.2.7.
5. Calvin, *Institutes*, 3.2.7.

ride. I enjoyed the beauty of the boat and wind and sea, but that appreciation did not get the boat or me to Rhode Island any more than my ardor and order—the Captain did.

Our capacity for understanding God no less than our sincerity and aesthetic sensibility may and can and does fail us. God never fails. God's love is independent of our capacity or will or depth. And because it is, we are freed from the incessant burden of measuring the sincerity and obedience of our faith. God's love allows us to forego anxious preoccupation with our*selves*. And that is good news for people looking around from the edge. When not staring at our feet we may actually enjoy the dance.

FOLLOWING

Faith by itself, if it has no works, is dead. —Jas 2:17

Faith does not change God; faith changes us. Faith moves us out of ourselves and toward God. A theocentric faith shifts the focus from us and directs us to the world God is remaking. The New Testament variously defines faith's response as following Jesus; obeying his word; abiding in him; bearing fruit; and, among other expressions, doing his works. When James wrote that faith without works was dead he did so to counter two misrepresentations: (1) faith is a matter of correct thinking, and (2) faith is a religious sentiment which allows us to leave the world for an hour or so on Sunday mornings only to return unfazed. Even if James is less explicit than some New Testament writers, he is clear that faith is God's gift. "In his own purpose," James reasons, "[God] gave us birth by the word of truth, so that we would become a kind of first fruits of his creatures" (Jas 1:18).

James took particular exception to class distinctions dividing the nascent Christian community. Disturbed by wealthy followers who displayed no empathy, he mockingly derided their treatment of the poor, "Go in peace, keep warm and eat your fill." Dismayed by the piously orthodox, James sarcastically raged, "You believe God is one; you do well. Even the demons believe—and shudder" (Jas 2:16, 19). Faith changes us. If God is kindly disposed toward us, how can we be any less kindly disposed toward others? The arc of faith moves us in love toward others and the shared living space we call Earth.

Paul insisted that faith radically reorients those who follow. "[P]resent your bodies as a living sacrifice," Paul urged his readers in Rome. "Do not be conformed to this world, but be transformed by the renewing of your minds, so that you may discern what is the will of God . . . " (Rom 12:1–2).

Paul likened transformation to death and resurrection. A radical predicament demands radical intervention. Our plight requires more than a gentle nudge, a bit of tweaking, life coaching, or better information. We need a new self, which is why Paul couches transformation in terms of new creation. Our predicament in the Anthropocene Epoch is not minor. We do not need extrication; we need a newly made orientation. We are not the center—the Creator and Redeemer is the center. And because God is the Center we may live as stewards and guests, not masters and owners.

Faith is a set of beliefs, a stance expressed as friendship with God birthed by God's love, which brings to mind a warning Jesus issued in the Sermon on the Mount. After cautioning listeners about the dangers of heeding wolf-like "false prophets" dressed in sheep's clothing who are detected by the "fruit" they bear, Jesus makes this warning: "Not everyone who says to me, 'Lord, Lord,' will enter the kingdom of heaven, but only the one who does the will of my Father in heaven" (Matt 7:21–22). To insure that his listeners heard correctly Jesus added preachers, exorcists, and miracle workers to his list of suspects. Religious activities, no less than religious appearances, can be deceiving.

Don't be fooled, Jesus seems to be saying; and don't fool yourself. He concluded his sermon with these words, "Everyone then who hears these words of mine and acts on them will be like a wise man who built his house on rock. The rain fell, the floods came, and the winds blew and beat on that house, but it did not fall because it had been founded on rock" (Matt 7:24–25). The crowds were astounded and no wonder because we are clever when building on the faulty foundations of our works and words and the ardor and order we bring to them. To survive wind and flood we need a different foundation—not our works and words or experiences but the bedrock of God's love. We need a theocentric foundation.

We do not trust our trust. We trust God's love. God's love not only withstands life's storms but sends us ready and able to love as we are loved. Faith does not leave us frail and needy, tossed to and fro, forever suspended in childish dependency. God is not interested in meeting us only at our wit's end or when we have exhausted all other possibilities or when we are disabled as if darkness and disability leave or prepare space for God to fit in or fill vacancies in our otherwise full and healthy lives. God meets us at the center and not as an added extra or bonus. God is the center "who gives life to the dead and calls into existence the things that do not exist" (Rom 4:17). A faith like that is not something we give ourselves. To use Paul's language, faith is a work of the Spirit "bearing witness with our spirit that we are children of God" (Rom 8:16). Likewise, John insisted that we become children of God "not by blood or of the will of the flesh or of the will of man, but of

God" (John 1:13). Or again, as Jesus observed of Peter when he confessed his faith, "flesh and blood has not revealed this to you, but my Father in heaven" (Matt 16:17).

Given that faith is a gift we cannot give ourselves, where or how do we receive and keep it? On multiple occasions Jesus answered that question this way, "If any want to become my followers, let them take up their cross and follow me" (Matt 16:24). It is curious that Jesus did not say, Go to church and listen to a sermon, nor for that matter did he suggest reading a book like this one or enrolling in a religion course or participating in a weekend spiritual retreat, not that retreats and classrooms and churches and even books cannot become places where we discover faith. Jesus says that we have faith when we follow where he goes, which means walking among and with the poor, the sick, the hungry, the oppressed; outcasts, prostitutes, prodigal deadbeats, drunkards and gluttons; hypocrites, rich folks trapped by their riches; and just about anybody else you can name in the human family. Faith is received where Jesus resides.

Friendship with God is formed when we live as Jesus lived—showing mercy, doing justice, loving kindness; forgiving others; breaking bread at table; retreating alone to mountaintops, keeping the Sabbath with others; and, when required, knocking heads with political and religious authorities. We are not Jesus, but when we follow him and live as he lived for others we will receive a faith worth having and keeping. A faith like that is an expression of grace, a topic for the next chapter.

Chapter 4

What Is Grace?

SURPRISED BY GRACE

He will separate people one from another as a shepherd separates the sheep from the goats. —Matt 25:32

Are you a righteous sheep or an unrighteous goat? According to Jesus, the last judgment will be full of surprise. There are sheep who do not know they are sheep and there are goats who do not know they are goats. Grace upends everything—most especially our notions of right and righteousness.

New York University Professor Jonathan Haidt's 2012 publication, *The Righteous Mind: Why Good People Are Divided by Politics and Religion*, became a national best seller reviving a term once reserved for cool '55 Chevys or less than cool or not cool *church ladies*. Contrary to the term's checkered usage, Haidt argues that we all want to be righteous or more commonly—right. And, what is more—we can't help it. Righteousness, so Haidt proposes, is a by-product of our DNA and the social environments we inhabit.

Righteousness is a uniquely human marker. Squid don't worry about it—people, well, we are another story. We are driven to be right—mainly, so Haidt argues, by intuition and secondarily by reason. Haidt's metaphor is an elephant rider. As he describes it, "*the mind is divided, like a rider on an elephant and the rider's job is to serve the elephant.*"[1] The rider, says Haidt, is conscious reason and the elephant "the other 99 percent" of our "mental

---

1. Haidt, *The Righteous Mind*, xxi. Emphasis original.

processes—the ones that occur outside of awareness."[2] Reasoned argument, Haidt maintains, follows unconscious drivers.

Haidt identifies six unconscious drivers or what he calls *taste receptors* which reside in the elephant: care/harm, fairness/cheating, loyalty/betrayal, authority/subversion, sanctity/degradation, and liberty/oppression.[3] These adaptive traits which sponsor survival are "prewired" in us, and, in Haidt's view, are variously expressed in and shaped by culture. Everyone wants to be *righteous*. Or, more precisely, by virtue of our humanity, we all are *righteous*—at least in our own minds. And gauging by cable TV news, we are only too happy to boast about it, which would not be such a big deal if the shouting was not indicative of matters important to human well-being, ranging from who cuts the pie to the size of each slice.

The desire to be right goes to the heart of what makes us human—we are moral actors, creatures of dust and breath, which brings me back to Jesus' parable: why the surprise on judgment day? Because the righteous did not know they were righteous and those who thought they were righteous discovered they were not righteous. According to Jesus, the identity of sheep and goats is hidden and known only to God. Judgment belongs to God and not to us, which may become a great gift. But that is one big *if*, because we are stuck on the righteousness we give ourselves. Surrendering our righteousness for the righteousness of God is a steep hill to climb.

THE GIFT OF LIFE

What do you have that you did not receive? —1 Cor 4:7

Paul makes this observation when parsing the pecking order that dominated the first-century Christian community at Corinth. He believed his Macedonian charges had it wrong. Contrary to their rendering, grace does not create privilege. The Corinthians relished a kind of spiritual Olympics, which may be understandable in as much as Athens was sixty miles away, but for Paul the leap was absurd. No one is a little bit Christian (or a little more Christian). Christians become Christians by virtue of God's judgment, which means that Christians are not classified. Whatever gifts we have are gifts we have been given. Gifts may be received or declined or received and not used or misused, but that does not make them any less given. How can we claim credit for what is given? And to Paul's mind, what we have been given is pretty much everything, not only the grace which saves us, grace

2. Haidt, *The Righteous Mind*, xxi.
3. Haidt, *The Righteous Mind*, xxi.

which makes us righteous or justified, but also talents given in service of the common good, indeed, life itself. Grace made us and newly remakes us. Of course that is hard to hear and gladly receive when busily advocating our own righteousness. We fight over righteousness no less than we fight over possessions, which is to say, until our last breath. Possessions and righteousness fit hand in glove. And why wouldn't they? Both secure survival. Both testify, we imagine, to our honor and ability and good fortune. A compelling story told by Luke (Luke 12:13–21) invites reflection regarding these troublesome twins which are energized and accompanied by notions of earning and deserving.

One day a man asked Jesus to settle a squabble over inheritance. Jesus declined insisting that arbitration was not his job. Jesus then warned the man and his brother about the dangers of greed, telling them that life "does not consist in the abundance of possessions." To persuade and prod his listeners, Jesus told a parable about a rich farmer whose land produced a bumper crop. The surplus created a problem because the farmer was short on storage. Not to worry, the farmer had a solution: bigger barns. Not only that, the wealthy farmer made a promise: he would enjoy life. He had earned the right. He deserved it: "You have ample goods laid up for many years; relax, eat, drink, be merry."

Sound familiar? It is the kind of thing we tell ourselves after years on the job. We put in our time. We spent wisely. We saved. We are set, fixed, ready to enjoy the good life. Sounds like a plan. Who would not want that? We suspect a punch line is coming, and it is. In the dead of night, God wakes the farmer from an otherwise peaceful sleep, disturbing him with a haunting question, "The things you have prepared, whose will they be?"

Look around. What will happen to all of your stuff? The beautiful walnut dining room furniture that belonged to your great-grandmother will go to your eldest. The clock on the mantel that your father gave your mother will pass to the younger. After retiring obligations, whatever remains will be divided; what else? Well, there is your legacy. There is that; it might be something grand like a school you helped build for children in Africa or, more modestly, fond memories of you carried by your former students, or the picture of you on your grandson's office credenza. "The things you have prepared, whose will they be?"

Jesus arrests attention with what everybody knows: life is more than possessions, and even those few or many we have we cannot take with us, which is a curiosity because we cling to them so tightly. You would think we know better, but somehow we don't. Job had it right, "Naked I came from my mother's womb, and naked I shall return there" (Job 1:21). It is the second half of Job's testimony that is more vexing and yet full of promise:

"The LORD gave, and the LORD has taken away; blessed be the name of the LORD" (Job 1:21) Or, as Jesus concluded to the farmer and his brother and whoever overheard, "So it is with those who store up treasures for themselves but are not rich toward God."

What makes for riches toward God? For starters, life requires a heap of humility and a great dose of gratitude. Grace not only surprises but also enables us to loosen our grip. When grace is received, all debts are off. We are forgiven.

THE GIFT OF RIGHTEOUSNESS

Since all have sinned and fall short of the glory of God; they are justified by his grace as a gift through the redemption that is in Christ.
—Rom 3:23

Are there debts we cannot pay? I am not talking about those we can pay like bumping into a stranger whose coffee spills and stains a starched white shirt. *Oh, I'm terribly sorry*, we say, reaching for our wallet. *Here, let me make it up to you.* The stranger says, *No bother.* And we say, *Please, I insist.* Was the twenty so we could walk away or so the stranger could clean his shirt? Even debts we pay are not without stain. What about those we can't pay, ones that shake us in the night—the hidden, secret sins we pray never see the light of day?

Haidt ends his book with an appeal for the righteous to "disagree more constructively," reasoning that to understand the mess we are in we must try to "understand why some people bind themselves to the liberal team, some to the conservative team, some to other teams or to no team at all."[4] As a child of the Enlightenment I too applaud the power of understanding difference. Reasoning together is far better than spoils going to victors even when reasoned arguments won leave their own kind of spoils. Our predicament is such that even reasonable people who disagree constructively bring hurt and harm, leaving debts that none can pay. If reason were the solution, Jesus might have distributed gold-leaf, leather-bound books instead of giving his life on a cross between thieves. Our hunger and thirst for the righteousness we earn and deserve must die. To use Haidt's terms, the elephant and its rider must die. Paul said it this way, "We know that our old self was crucified with him so that the body of sin might be destroyed, and we might no longer be enslaved to sin" (Rom 6:6). The old self is the self that demands that God judge us based on our merits, our deserving, our goodness, even our faith

---

4. Haidt, *The Righteous Mind*, 321.

and faithfulness. The new self birthed by the Spirit acknowledges that we are saved by grace.

Peter had a problem. What about sin? Not his sin, but somebody who sinned against him. What should he do? Peter consulted Jesus. It's sufficient, isn't it, Jesus, if I let them off seven times? That's enough, right? That will do, won't it? Jesus replied, "Not seven times, but I tell you, seventy times seven." Maybe Peter looked pleased, more likely puzzled which prompted Jesus to compare the kingdom of heaven to a king who discovered a slave who owed a debt larger than anyone could pay (Matt 18:21–35). The king ordered the slave sold, together with his wife and children and all of his possessions. What is a slave to a king?

The slave fell on his knees and begged for mercy promising to repay everything. Out of pity the king released the slave from the unpayable debt. A short time later the forgiven slave ran into a fellow slave who owed him a small sum. The debtor pled for mercy. The forgiven slave grabbed him by the throat. The debtor continued begging for mercy but the forgiven slave threw him into jail. Witnesses to the exchange informed the king, who summoned the unyielding forgiven slave. "You wicked slave," the king declared. "I forgave you all that debt because you pleaded with me. Should you not have had mercy on your fellow slave, as I had mercy on you?" In his anger, the king handed the man over to be tortured, until he paid the entire debt. "So," said Jesus, "my heavenly Father will also do to every one of you, if you do not forgive your brother or sister from your heart."

Do not seize upon the image of a heavenly jailer, or do linger there if it rattles settled conceptions of a benign Heavenly Father who sleeps or overlooks injustice. Better still; consider debts that can't be paid—not just the ones you owe but also those owed to you. How can any get out till the last penny is paid? The short answer is, we cannot—not separate and apart from radical intervention. "All have sinned and fall short," not just of "the glory of God" but of the debts we cannot repay. "[W]e are justified by God's grace as a gift." The righteousness we have is not our own. The righteousness we have belongs to Christ and is given to us free of charge.[5]

It sounds too good to be true—debts forgiven, mercy for all? What about fairness and justice, earning and deserving, reward and punishment, right and wrong? Is righteousness transferrable? And why do the right thing, especially when it is costly? If in the end, judgment belongs to God and not to us, why strive, why care, why bother? Christopher Morse, referencing Paul, addresses this concern. "[R]ighteousness is the faithfulness of God— that is, who God is as trustworthy keeper of the commitment to make all

---

5. Volf, *Free of Charge*, 55–87.

things right and to vindicate the right in all things."[6] This righteousness, as Morse explains, "is not propositional information . . . but a personal, committed Self who becomes known not as *something* but as *Someone* who keeps faith with us."[7] We keep faith because God keeps faith. We do not trust our faith; we trust God's faithfulness to "make all things right and to vindicate the right in all things."

The most amazing thing about grace is not the fear it relieves but the fear it teaches, fear before the wondrous righteous compassion of the God who made us, "who does not deal with us according to our sins . . . he remembers that we are dust" (Ps 103:10, 14). The amazing thing about grace is that our Judge is also our Redeemer and Creator.

Rather than fighting about who is right or being right we are better served by sharing the grace we have received. And grace is received when and as it is given; or, as Jesus taught disciples to pray, "Forgive us our debts, as we also forgive our debtors" (Matt 6:12). We pray daily because grace is newly given each day. The relentless love of God for his creation creates perseverance and persistence. Enabled by God's grace we passionately pursue forgiving debtors. "The steadfast love of the LORD never ceases," Jeremiah says, "his mercies never come to an end; they are new every morning" (Lam 3:22–23). Grace is the one "pearl of great price" for which we search again and again and upon finding it we will sell everything we have (Matt 13:46).

Bonhoeffer observed in his book, *The Cost of Discipleship*, that there is a kind of "cheap grace," which presumes that since all debts are paid in advance, we may presume upon grace and merely blend in the world, taking a path of least resistance, substituting blissful ignorance or indifferent tolerance for the costly work of reconciliation.[8]

Grace is not another word for hand-holding while singing *Kumbaya* on somnolent Sunday mornings. Grace, which is "the power of God for salvation" (Rom 1:16) sends and equips us to struggle with and for others amidst contested rights that too often accrue debts that cannot be paid, except by costly forgiveness. Grace does not give a wink and a nod to the consequences of sin. There is justice in justification. Grace makes us righteous, not the righteousness we give ourselves, but the righteousness which comes from God which is given and sought daily.

We are never finished with grace. Grace teaches our hearts to fear. Grace makes us anxious to please God, not ourselves. Paul put it this way, "By the grace of God I am what I am, and his grace toward me has not been

---

6. Morse, *Not Every Spirit*, 102.
7. Morse, *Not Every Spirit*, 102.
8. Bonhoeffer, *The Cost of Discipleship*, 43–56.

in vain. On the contrary, I worked harder than any of them—though it was not I, but the grace of God that is with me" (1 Cor 15:10).

Grace, while teaching our hearts to fear, does not leave us dangling, feverishly questioning our standing with God. Grace does not leave us frozen, inept, cowering, and afraid of offending an Arbitrary Unknown. Sin, which makes cowards of us all, most especially before God, is vanquished by grace, by the good news of Jesus Christ. While we do not presume upon grace, grace stands us upon rock, filling us with courage and good hope. By grace we may greet each day anew, as the dawning of the first day, because each day mercy freshly springs from the life-giving well of God's kindness.

God's kindness makes us bold. Kindness makes us persevere. Kindness keeps us from walking over the edge so that we walk in the light of God's day. Kindness allows us to abide in the righteousness of God's grace which arrests striving and earning and deserving and brings joyful confidence in the faithfulness of God. Righteousness given by God relocates us. It moves us from the center so that we may live outwardly for others in grace as stewards of our home, Earth. The arc of this grace-filled relocation will be traced in the chapters that follow beginning with inspiration and direction for living righteously by grace as uniquely found in the testimony of Scripture, "a lamp to our feet" (Ps 119:105), the focus of the next chapter.

Chapter 5

What Is The Bible?

THE BOOKS

Whatever was written in former days was written for our instruction, so that by steadfastness and by the encouragement of the scriptures we might have hope. Rom 15:4

In the previous two chapters we explored how through *faith alone* and *grace alone* we might enjoy durable freedom to tend the garden and honor the One in whose image we are made. In this chapter we will explore how *Scripture alone* inspires, measures, and guides this life.

The Bible—a singular noun in English, from a plural Greek and Latin noun translated *the books*, alternately known as the Holy Bible, the Holy Scriptures, or colloquially as the Book or the Good Book—is a collection of sixty-six books (a number agreed by most Protestants anyway) written principally in Hebrew and Greek with a touch of Aramaic between roughly 1000 BCE and 150 CE by forty-plus writers and editors depending on who does the counting. Chapter divisions were added in the thirteenth century; verses came in the sixteenth. The oldest complete Bible, *Codex Vaticanus*, dating from 300 to 325 CE and written on vellum or calf-skin, also termed parchment, is preserved in the Vatican Library where it first appeared five hundred years ago. No one knows how it got there though when it arrived some of its roughly ten-by-ten-inch pages or folios were missing. Most were there—759 out of an estimated 820. The missing pages were added to *Codex*

Vaticanus soon after it arrived when other ancient manuscripts were used to supply the missing pages.

The Bible is an old book and not only ancient but in many ways strange to twenty-first-century readers. Just how old and how strange is partly a function of perspective. Compared to yesterday's news, the Bible seems very old and the gap between then and now large. As a child I was intrigued by the art displayed in our family Bible. Works, like Ruben's seventeenth-century Flemish Baroque rendering of Eden, were a particular curiosity. Why is Adam sitting under an apple tree? Why is Eve standing and handing him fruit? And why are they naked? Why is a fat snake coiled in the tree? Why are the animals watching? It was a world like no other—the strange world of the Bible.

Perspective is partly a function of framing. What happens to our perception of the Bible's age if we place it in a larger time frame? Imagine compressing the last two hundred thousand years into one calendar year. Anatomically modern humans appeared around two hundred thousand years ago; Abraham left Uruk roughly four thousand years ago. Using a one-year time scale, humans appeared 365 days ago while Father Abraham arrived in Canaan just seven days ago. Using this time frame, Abraham is not nearly as ancient as we ordinarily imagine. What happens if we use an even larger frame?

History Professor David Christian scales our 13.8 billion-year-old universe into 13.8 years. Using this scale the stars appeared 13.2 years ago; our solar system 4.5 years ago; Earth's earliest life forms 3.9 years ago; the extinction of the dinosaurs twenty-four days ago; anatomically modern humans one hundred minutes ago; agriculture five minutes ago; the Roman Empire one minute ago; the fossil fuels revolution six seconds ago; and humans landing on the moon—three seconds ago.[1] How ancient is Father Abraham now? Using Christian's time scale, Abraham lived about two minutes ago.

If these thought experiments close the gap between our time and Bible times, a gap still remains, a particularly difficult one, a cultural-linguistic gap.[2] Bridging that gap is not impossible, but it is something to keep before us when reading the Bible or any other ancient text and even some that are not so ancient.

I grew up in the 1950s and '60s. My six grandchildren can imaginatively enter that age by listening to my tales or by reading history or novels. They can listen to *Elvis* or *The Beatles* or *The Rolling Stones*. They can watch black-and-white episodes of *The Andy Griffith Show* or documentaries of

---

1. Christian, *Origin Story*, 12–14.
2. Lindbeck, *The Nature of Doctrine*, 130–34.

Apollo Eleven landing on the moon. Those things will help close the gap, but my grandchildren cannot know precisely what it felt like to be alive in those days. Simple things like the feel of walking to a corner grocery where sawdust covers the butcher counter floor are largely inaccessible to them.

The reverse is also true. I do not know what it feels like to be my grandchildren growing up in an increasingly crowded and wired world where most anything and everything that happens can be flashed most anywhere the moment it happens. Gaps like these do not make communication with my grandchildren impossible. In many ways cultural-linguistic differences enrich our relationships, but the differences between my times and theirs remain. Cultural-linguistic differences are even more pronounced when gaps are greater, like the one between our time and say, 1492 CE. Imagine then the amplified differences between our time and those depicted in the Bible. How do we enter that world when it is not only distant but strangely different from ours?

While imaginative time travel is not impossible, navigation requires recognizing that the world of Abraham and Moses and Jesus is not the world of 1965 much less the year we occupy now. Mindful of this gap I invite you to think about the Bible as spoken; written; a word or the Word made flesh; and, finally, the word of God that is near, heard, and lived.

SPOKEN

Then God said, 'Let there be light'; and there was light. —Gen 1:3

Read the book of Deuteronomy or re-read it and notice the identity of the speaker. The first sentence tells readers that they are about to read "words that Moses spoke" to Israel in the wilderness beyond the Jordan. Six verses later the speaker is God. And so it goes throughout thirty-four chapters up to and including the moment when God speaks a last word before Moses takes his final breath. The speaking voice in Deuteronomy switches back and forth between Moses and God lending literary credence to the expression that the Bible is the word of God.

Imagine hearing a sermon—or perhaps you have heard one—where the preacher insists that she is not speaking about God or on God's behalf but is the voice of God. No distinctions are drawn between the preacher's voice and God's voice. They are one. This is the imagined world of Deuteronomy, the core of which was likely written sometime during King Josiah's reign (640–609 BCE) some six hundred years after the time of Moses and the Exodus.

My interest is not history or the historical veracity of Deuteronomy. My interest is how Deuteronomy exemplifies a primary purpose of the Bible which Deuteronomy affirms not only in form but content. That purpose is disclosed in a concluding speech by Moses: "Assemble the people—men, women, and children, as well as the aliens residing in your towns—so that they may hear and learn to fear the LORD your God and to observe diligently all the words of this law, and so that their children, who have not known it, may hear and learn to fear the LORD your God" (Deut 31:12–13). The Bible aims to make God known in order to inspire, measure, and guide a people. The medium is language, both spoken and written.

Any account of what makes us human must consider language. How our ancestors acquired language between and 100,000 and 250,000 years ago remains unclear. What is beyond dispute is that by some seventy thousand years ago our ancestors spoke about a near world which included things like trees, wind, and neighbors. They also spoke about an unseen, imagined world filled with animal spirits and other complex abstractions such as tribe, nation, and coinage. The Bible, a recent newcomer in this long story, offers profound though not singular evidence of a unique feature of being human—communication through words spoken and written. Extraordinary as that is, the Bible's framing of the creation of the universe as an utterance by God is singularly stunning. According to Genesis, God *speaks* and creation is created. God's speaking not only inspires, measures, and guides; it creates.

WRITTEN

Jesus did many other signs in the presence of his disciples, which are not written in this book. —John 20:30

If speaking is a function of the mouth and ear, writing is a function of hand and eye, which is to acknowledge that writing embodies seen and unseen realities. Ten thousand years ago humans began cutting marks in soft clay tablets to represent reality. Through pictographs and other symbols Sumerians kept track of trade goods, livestock, and other sundries such as land management. Cuneiform writing, the earliest known form of writing was painstaking, highly skilled, and transformative. Writing allowed abstractions to become physical and thereby not only portable but less subject to the vicissitudes of time. Thanks to writing we know large portions of our ancestors' story. Ensuing centuries would see expanded and refined means of fixing and transporting the seen and unseen; consider the revolution started by Johannes Gutenberg in the mid-fifteenth century.

Gutenberg's movable-type printing press helped usher in the modern world. The tool he invented to embody abstraction was central not only to the Renaissance, Reformation, and the Scientific Revolution but also to critical learning among non-landed people, which included just about everybody who formerly was nobody.

J. K. Rowling's *Harry Potter* series has been translated into eighty languages. Some 500 million copies have been sold, making it the world's second most read book. The Bible holds first place with over five *billion* copies published and translated into 670 languages. Speaking of a medium for transporting seen and unseen realities; no other book is more widely available than the Bible which may inspire, measure, and guide life which brings this written abstraction to the Word made flesh.

MADE FLESH

In the beginning was the Word. . . . And the Word became flesh and lived among us. —John 1:1, 14

If speaking is a function of mouth and ear and writing a function of hand and eye, how do we narrate or account or describe an announcement that the Word which spoke the universe into being was made flesh and blood? Asked another way, how do we talk about the medium which makes us human becoming not just a function of a mouth and ear or hand and eye, but a flesh-and-blood human?

I did not know my parental grandfather. He died two years before I was born. I say I did not know him; more precisely, I never met him. He died two years before I was born. I came to know him by observing and listening to my father and his five siblings. At their holiday and summertime gatherings they frequently told stories about Roby Thomas Sinclair or *RT*, the name I most often heard used in reference to my grandfather whose black and white image bore a striking resemblance, at least to my young mind, to his contemporary, President Franklin D. Roosevelt. Though I never met *RT* I know that he was witty and quick-tempered. He was old for his age, not particularly athletic but bright and industrious. He was a railroad company freight officer who managed to send all six of his children through college and this despite two world wars and the Great Depression. I have a gold pocket watch, minus the chain, that my grandfather carried and a steamer trunk identified by his name artfully scratched into one of five ornamental oak straps decorating its lid. I do not know where my grandfather traveled with that steamer, perhaps up and down the Atlantic Coast Line Railroad, but it is a daily presence of him in my home.

Stories, photos, personal effects, knowledge of historical setting, and more importantly living witnesses, help us know about persons who lived in the past. However helpful and accurate these instruments may be in making the past present they cannot substitute for having actually known someone by living daily with them. That is the extraordinary testimony of the Bible. The invisible Word of God once spoken and written, the Word which spoke all things into existence was made flesh. One first-century witness expressed this amazing claim in these words, "We declare to you what was from the beginning, what we have heard, what we have seen with our eyes, what we have looked at and touched with our hands, concerning the word of life—this life was revealed . . ." (1 John 1:1-2). John was talking about Jesus of Nazareth, not just a wise teacher or a wonder-worker or a prophet, but the Word which brought us into being, the Word made flesh and blood in a Jewish rabbi crucified by the imperial Roman governor, Pontius Pilate.

The Word of God is not just an idea or written abstraction or a spoken rendering of imagined unseen reality. The Word of God became a human being. The testimony of Scripture is that if you and I want to understand who God is and what God is like we should see Jesus. Seeing Jesus mitigates guesswork. Hebrews described Jesus this way, "He is the reflection of God's glory and the exact imprint of God's very being . . ." (Heb 1:3). Or as Paul put it, "He is the image of the invisible God . . ." (Col 1:15).

The Bible claims that the Word became flesh. How do we know this and how do we know it to be true? The Bible anticipates this question and answers in these words, "Now Jesus did many other signs in the presence of his disciples, which are not written in this book. But these are written so that you may come to believe that Jesus is the Messiah, the Son of God, and that through believing you may have life in his name" (John 20:30-31). According to John, we "have life" by reading about Jesus. Paul, a generation earlier adds another means—life in Christ comes by hearing (Rom 10:14-17). Again, we are back to reading and hearing, language functions of the eye and ear. The Bible goes a step further—the Word of God is also written on human hearts. That kind of writing is classically defined as the work of the Spirit. The Bible inspires us. The Bible inspires us not because it is infallible, inerrant, or unassailable truth. The Bible inspires because the Bible is a human word through which God speaks. Citing the Bible's many anthropomorphisms Calvin referred to the Bible as baby talk. Through Scripture, God accommodates to us, speaking to us as a nurse might "lisp" to infants.[3]

LIVED

The word is very near you; it's in your mouth and in your heart for you to observe. —Deut 30:14

Later in the passage cited above, Moses insists that the word of God is not "too hard" for us nor "too far away." Paul, echoing Moses, persuades that you and I are not able to go to heaven to bring God down any more than we can ascend to the abyss to bring God up (Rom 10:6–7), which makes a compelling case for the idea that understanding God is not a matter of time travel as if to say that the purpose of reading and hearing the Bible is to *get back* to its times so that our recovery efforts enable us to understand God or somehow make the Bible relevant. Those efforts help, but the Bible insists that the Word of God comes to us—spoken, written, and made flesh. That Word is heard and inscribed and made alive by the kindness of God's Spirit. We are not able to conjure or summon or make the Word of God relevant. The Word comes to and inspires us.

God comes to us in a human and sometimes all too human way. We should not be embarrassed by this humiliation. The Bible is a humble word. We need not apologize for it or smooth out its rough edges so that it conforms to our present abstracted understandings. Our task is responding to the spoken, written, and lived Word which inspires, measures, and guides our living. That has been God's purpose all along, "to write his word upon our hearts" not so that we become blind puppets marching to heavenly orders but fully alive and newly made human beings whose living reflects God's glory to the well-being of God's creation. Before fleshing out this lived response we will pause briefly in the next chapter to consider the relationship between science and religion.

---

3. Calvin, *Institutes*, 1.13.1.

Chapter 6

Creation or Evolution?

LAUREN AND MARGARET

Ever since the creation of the world his eternal power and divine nature, invisible though they are, have been understood and seen through the things he has made. —Rom 1:20

Lauren and Margaret have known each other forever. Their parents, college graduates and professionals, also know one another. They know many of the same people, attend the same church, and send their daughters to the same school where Lauren and Margaret are college-bound eleventh-grade honor students. Lauren and Margaret imagine professional careers, engineering and medicine respectively. They are bright, energetic, happy, and responsible to a fault. A day will come when their imagined futures will come true.

On a day before that day, Lauren and Margaret were in Sunday school. That was not unusual. Lauren and Margaret were regulars. On this Sunday the lesson morphed into conversation about religion and science, specifically creation and evolution. The turn was not the teacher's intention, but she welcomed it. The Sunday school teacher was not anxious with youth. They were her life. Providing a secure space for exploration was her custom. The teacher's affection was genuine as her methods were skilled.

I don't want to think about it, Lauren winced. I just can't do evolution.

Sounds like a God thing to me, Margaret smiled. Can we also talk about the Big Bang?

Time cannot be turned back any more than the knowledge genie can be squeezed into its lamp. Two hundred years ago Lauren and Margaret might have chatted before class about the newly adopted American flag with thirteen stripes and twenty-one stars or had they overheard family dinner conversation they may have whispered worries about a looming financial panic that shook the world in 1819. Conversation about evolution would have to wait forty years but when it arrived, did it ever arrive. In recent generations few intersections between religion and science have been more contentious.

Let's talk about Lauren's worries and Margaret's welcome. What should a person of faith or someone of uncertain faith or no expressed faith do with evolution and more generally with the discipline of science here in the epoch of the Anthropocene? In brief, people of faith may welcome the light of science, including the science of evolution while people of science may welcome the light of religion. Before illustrating my own welcome through readings of creation narratives in Genesis, let me first identify two approaches which are less than helpful; one pertains to science, the other to religion. Both are anxiety driven. Nowhere has this anxiety been more clearly displayed than in shouting debates between religionists and scientists over creation. Perhaps we should expect such dustups. Then again, it may be that contrary to past experience these two paths of knowledge may labor together. But first, let's pull some anxiously growing weeds in each field. I will start with religion.

Increasingly since the turn of the twentieth century, religionists have typically used one of two strategies to cope with the advance of science when reading the Bible and making public claims about its meaning and significance. Each strategy attempts to make the Bible trustworthy. For their part conservatives steadfastly and fundamentalists more stridently have read the Bible as chronicle or history of events. Liberals, on the other hand, have countered the perceived threat to the Bible's trustworthiness with notions of myth or universal structures of truth. I met this second strategy as a college freshman when my university professor of Old Testament introduced Genesis as myth. Without alternatives I responded with alarm. The professor's strategy clashed with my strategy. Did he just say Genesis was a myth? Does he not believe the Bible is true? He must be of the devil. While fifty years later I have moved away from conservative strategies and more toward my professor's, I do not believe the trustworthiness of the Bible is established with reference to either chronicle or myth. The Bible is better understood as testimony, proclamation, covenantal witness, and the like. The division of the Bible into either myth or chronicle does not advance faithful understanding.

The writer of Hebrews said best what I am trying to say, "By faith we understand that the worlds were prepared by the word of God, so that what is seen was made from things that are not visible" (Heb 11:3). The Bible is testimony to the Creator who creates creation. Testimony is made "through faith for faith."

At their ordination Presbyterian leaders are asked nine questions, among them: "Do you accept the Scriptures of the Old and New Testaments to be, by the Holy Spirit, the unique and authoritative witness to Jesus Christ in the Church universal, and God's Word to you?"[1] When leaders answer affirmatively they attest to the trustworthiness of the Bible. They make a confession of faith. While leaders may hold particular understandings of inspiration and while they may variously interpret Scripture as chronicle or myth or otherwise, those understandings and methods follow or proceed from faith. "Faith seeks understanding." Faith is prior to understanding otherwise faith is not only unnecessary but also disposed along with "the author and finisher" of faith (Hebrews 12:2 KJV).

Faith is prior to understanding. Equally important, faith is determined by its subject. Such is the case not only for religion but also science. Among Christians the subject is God. Among scientists the subject is the natural world.

Scientists have a basic faith that the world is knowable otherwise their efforts are absurd. Scientists also trust their methods. Why bother counting things like quarks if quantification does not lend trustworthy support to understanding? Additionally, without faith or something akin to intuition how do scientists know where to begin looking for things like quarks and other intriguing curiosities? When breaking ground and when growing results, science proceeds by faith—a faith determined by its subject.[2]

Scientists and religionists alike live by faith. While each discipline possesses grammar and methodologies suited for the purpose of its inquiry, each enterprise begins with a faith governed by its subject which is deemed trustworthy. Both disciplines are susceptible to every limitation of our humanity, including anxiety. Religion errs when it appeals to the authority of eternal and objective truth whether as chronicle or myth. If the truth about God was assessable by reason alone, faith would be irrelevant and unnecessary as would God.

Science, for its part, stumbles when it appeals to reified facts presumed to be objective and somehow miraculously unstained by human observation. Things are unknowable in themselves. All knowledge, whether of God

---

1. Presbyterian Church (U.S.A.), *Book of Order*, W-4003b.
2. Polanyi, *Personal Knowledge*, 285–86.

or the natural world, is filtered and we are the filter. Theory attempts to ameliorate or remove observer bias but never succeeds entirely.[3] Science errs when it quells the anxiety to be filter-less by asserting that its claims are neutral quantifications and not theory-laden social constructs supported by layered institutional props ranging from peer review to government and corporate funding.[4] Scientific knowledge no less than religious knowledge is human whether expressed corporately or individually. In sum, both science and religion are founded upon a "confessional basis."[5]

The battle between science and religion need not be pitched or even a battle. Science and religion work best "in mutual modification."[6] Humankind needs both disciplines in order to construe truthful renderings of reality. With so much at stake in this epoch, it is incumbent that we recognize the contributions of both disciplines and welcome the prospect of vigorous continued conversation and "mutual modification." While each discipline pursues understanding with unique grammar and methods elicited by their respective subjects, both are human efforts. We do not have one self for knowing the natural world, and a second, differing self for knowing God. Said otherwise, Lauren does not need fear the theory of evolution while Margaret may pursue the promise and possibilities of science. Hopefully Lauren and Margaret will walk together and continue to listen. With this in view I invite you to consider two readings from Genesis.

A READING OF GENESIS 1:1—2:4

Then God said, "Let us make humankind in our image, according to our likeness." —Gen 1:26

The seven-day creation story, alternately known as the first creation account, accorded by its location in Scripture, announces God's sovereignty to those oppressed by coercive power. The good news of this testimony is that humans are raised to royal status by the Creator who makes them in his image and likeness. Readers hear the rhythmic liturgical call and response of this witness to God's sovereign love in the cadence of the poetry: God said, Let there be light and there was light. God said, Let there be a dome in the waters and there was a dome. God said, Let the earth bear fruit, and the earth bore fruit. And the heavens shouted Amen. Amen. Amen.

---

3. Polanyi, *Personal Knowledge*, 3–6.
4. Kuhn, *The Structure of Scientific Revolutions*, 176–91.
5. Nebelsick, *Theology and Science in Mutual Modification*, 175.
6. Nebelsick, *Theology and Science in Mutual Modification*, title page.

In the first creation story God lifts up defeated and despairing humanity. God creates humankind like God. Being God-like is an order different from being God. There is an infinite qualitative distinction or difference between God and God-like humans.[7] As Kierkegaard (1813–1855) put it, "God does not think, he creates; God does not exist, He is eternal. Man thinks and exists, and existence separates thought and being, holding them apart from one another in succession."[8] Or, as Genesis testifies, God speaks and creation is created.

God does not speak or act dispassionately or disinterestedly. The Creator notices creation—"It was good." That chorus chimes throughout the story. The Creator is satisfied that everything created is "very good" or "lovely, pleasing, beautiful."[9] Creation is not perfect, but good enough, a fit environment for God-like humans who are gifted by the Creator with a home. Earth is "very good" but "is not a state of perfection, not a static state of affairs."[10] Or, as Ecclesiastes says, "He has made everything *suitable* for its time . . ." (Eccl 3:11).

Creation is given, a givenness which is not scarce or partial but abundant—more than enough—a generous givenness that is ordered and therefore trustworthy, stable, changing, and nameable or knowable by its inhabitants.

The God-like ones are raised up to be fruitful and to multiply. They are commanded to subdue the earth and to have dominion over it. The command comes with a powerful caveat—the God-like ones are not owners of creation. Creation belongs to God. Creation is God's gift. Human subduing and domineering is a restricted, peculiar kind of ruling. Unlike the destroying and exploiting rule which makes exiles by tearing them from their home and despoiling their territory, human dominion is sanctioned to be akin to a shepherd's care or a farmer's watch. Human dominion is characterized by patience and long-suffering. Consider this kind of rule as you think about land use, resource management, energy production and consumption, and other human impacts on our shared living space, "a minuscule zone a few kilometers thick . . . biofilm, a varnish, a skin."[11] Think about this rule as you ponder industrial food production, gene manipulation, population, economics, and like issues. We have been given a precious gift; how should we watch over and care for it?

---

7. Kierkegaard, *Concluding Unscientific Postscript*, 266–322.

8. Kierkegaard, *Concluding Unscientific Postscript*, 269.

9. Brueggemann, *Genesis*, 37.

10. Fretheim, "Genesis," in Brueggeman et al., *General and Old Testament Articles*, 346.

11. Latour, *Down to Earth*, 78.

Human standing is achieved by God's gracious act of creation. We are not the center and yet we are not separate from creation. Human life is shared with green plants and creeping things and everything that has the breath of life. We are not the crowning moment of creation. God "finished" his work on the seventh day. Sabbath is the apogee, a blessed and hallowed day of rest.

On the seventh and final day of creation the Creator rested, not the exhausted sleep of anxious toil or a scarcity-driven, fretful fatigue. The Creator's rest is like the joy of an artisan satisfied with work that is good enough.[12] The seventh day is blessed and hallowed by the Creator's rested work and is given for God-like humans to rest as well, not sleeping, not fretting, but blessed and hallowed rest. Imagine that kind of rest—not just for humankind but also for the earth. The prospect and possibilities spill over with promise.

A READING OF GENESIS 2:4B—3:24

Then the LORD GOD said, "See, the man has become like one of us, knowing good and evil; and now, he might reach out his hand and take also from the tree of life, and eat and live forever. —Gen 3:22

The garden creation story or second creation account proclaims good news for humans but also a terrible warning—Godlikeness bears awful consequences when it is marred and distorted by grasping and reaching and betraying. The givenness of creation, the narrative tells, is disturbed by grasping and reaching and betraying. Readers know this when harsh words intrude into the narrative—words such as afraid, fear, naked, tricked, cursed, enmity, strike, toil, sweat, pangs, pain, thorns and thistles, rule over, evil, and death. Readers recognize turmoil in the garden when the entrance to the garden is blocked and guarded by a flaming, turning sword. Something in the garden is out of balance. Turmoil is fierce and roams disruptively.

If the seven-day creation story lifts up a conquered people, the garden story brings them back down to Earth. The Godlike ones are brought low when they cross a limit intended by God for their protection. The one fruit that was forbidden was forbidden because it was dangerous. When humans transgress their limit, distrust, deception, and betrayal enter the scene. The disruption disturbs not only us but also Earth from which we were taken and to which we return.

---

12. Brueggemann, *Genesis*, 37.

No less than in the first creation story, in this story God is the dynamic, central actor, which does not mean that humans are merely acted upon. We are actors in becoming like God, only the price of admission is greater than we can pay apart from grace. Genesis depicts grace as clothing provided by the Creator to cover shame brought about when a limit is crossed. Grace is shown by the Creator's prohibition that prevents humans from turning and living forever in their low estate. The sentence prevents and forestalls sudden death though death will come.

There are dire consequences when humans exceed limits. Grace, yes, but also consequence. Humans are not puppets. Integrating science and religion holds promise for staying within our limits and living constructively rather than destructively in the only environment we have. Like Father Abraham who laughed at the prospect of promise or Jacob who limped after his encounter with God, we walk with dis-ease east of Eden. With Moses sitting on the mountain edge overlooking a land he will not enter, so we live as sojourners in a strange land. It has always been this way. Ask Jeremiah who lamented or Isaiah who fell to the temple floor in awestruck fear. Speak with Peter who fled in the night after denying his friend or Paul who persecuted the One who wanted to save him. We, as they, walk "through faith for faith." We, as they, live as strangers and aliens as if in a foreign land. We live by grace through faith seeking the promise of Sabbath rest.

With others I do not read Genesis as chronicle or myth, but rather as testimony, witness, and proclamation of good news. We cannot get behind this ancient story to discern what it meant originally and we need not do that in order to hear a word from God or about God. We need only to let the story have its own voice to inform and reform our voice today. Rather than drawing conclusions about eternal truths or discerning historical events which are somehow determinative of the way things are today, we are better served by listening and allowing the story to have its way with us. That is a practiced art and devotion which will yield much for us here at the beginning of a daunting epoch when we must learn over and over again through each and all generations how it is that we are like God and how very different God is from us. Our lives depend on the answers we render. In the chapter that follows we will hear that the Creator has not and does not leave us to walk alone east of Eden. The Creator will come as reconciler and redeemer.

Chapter 7

Why Did Jesus Die?

STUMBLING BLOCK AND FOLLY

Let the Messiah, the King of Israel, come down from the cross now, so that we may see and believe. —Mark 15: 32

It is difficult to see a messiah or a king on a cross—much less God. If we had our way, Jesus would come down from the cross. Since he does not, we try to take him down. We try to remove Jesus from the cross. In the mid-first century, Paul identified these efforts as a demand for signs and a desire for wisdom. Each was advanced to overcome what Paul called the *stumbling block* and *folly* of the cross. To ancient Jews the cross looked like weakness. To Greeks it appeared to be folly. Summarizing these attempts and countering them Paul wrote: "We proclaim Christ crucified a stumbling block to Jews and foolishness to Gentiles, but to those who are called, both Jews and Greeks, Christ is the power of God and the wisdom of God" (1 Cor 1:22–25).

These well-traveled efforts are still in play. They are employed today, however, not by Jews or Greeks but by Christians. The first iteration may be found among sign-seeking fundamentalists, conservatives, and evangelicals. The second appears among wisdom-seeking moderates and liberals.

Stumbling over the weakness of the cross, sign-seekers interpret the cross as a plan of salvation necessitated by justice wrapped in a theory of atonement. Stumbling over the foolishness of the cross, wisdom-seekers interpret the cross as a moral exemplar worthy of imitation. Our stumbling is understandable. How can a God of absolute power, justice, and holiness be crucified as a weak, godless, and godforsaken criminal? How can an absolutely loving, faithful, and liberating God be crucified as a godless and godforsaken criminal who is hated, betrayed, and humiliated? Muscular readings of the cross no more remove stumbling than cerebral ones. "The power of God and the wisdom of God" are revealed through the weakness and folly of the cross."

THE CRUCIFIED GOD

My God, my God, why have you forsaken me? —Mark 15:34

Jesus did not die of natural causes. Unlike a Stoic philosopher or Zen master, Jesus did not die calmly, bravely, or serenely. He did not die as a religious martyr or tragic hero fighting a noble, lost cause. He did not die as a first responder on the scene of an accident or soldier lending aid to fallen brothers in arms. Jesus did not die admired or celebrated or venerated. He died betrayed, denied, and forsaken by his closest friends. He died mocked by imperial soldiers. He died derided by his ancestral people as a phony, godless blasphemer. But more than anything, he died forsaken by the Father he believed near, the One he called Abba who numbered the hairs on his head, the One who was ready to save and not judge. This One abandoned Jesus, *gave him up*, and left him twisting on a wooden beam to die. The cross is and remains good news when we refuse any and all efforts to take Jesus down from the cross. As Bonhoeffer observed from his Tegel prison cell: "only the suffering God can help."[1]

The suffering God who can help redefines "wisdom and power." Jesus does persuade by dazzling signs and he inspires with captivating moral wisdom. Jesus was a wise teacher and a wonder-worker. But ultimately the way of Jesus is the way of the cross. God redefines "wisdom and power" uniquely, exclusively, and particularly in Jesus of Nazareth who suffered under Pontius Pilate and was crucified.

In her compelling book Fleming Rutledge observes that "until the gospel of Jesus Christ burst upon the Mediterranean world, no one in the history of human imagination had conceived of such a thing as the worship of a crucified man."[2] I would add; no one previously imagined the worship of a crucified God. The oddness of the crucifixion was not lost on first-century witnesses as evidenced not only by Paul's Corinthian readers but also those

---

1. Bonhoeffer, *Letters & Papers from Prison*, 360.
2. Rutledge, *The Crucifixion*, 1.

of the Fourth Gospel living a generation later. In an extended discourse where Jesus tells his disciples that his flesh is the bread of life given for the world, the disciples respond, "This teaching is difficult; who can accept it?" The reaction prompted Jesus to ask, "Does this offend you?" (John 6:35–71). Two thousand years later the offense remains as does the difficulty.

When attempting to understand the crucifixion, though we may be accustomed to language about necessary plans of salvation or drawn by sensible language regarding moral wisdom, we are better served by following the instincts of the New Testament. That testimony, drawing upon a deep repertoire of metaphors, retains the weakness and folly of the cross. Among many expressions, four primary metaphors may be identified: financial, martial, sacrificial, and legal.[3]

New Testament witnesses variously invite listeners to imaginatively enter a slave market, battlefield, temple, and courtroom. In the market they are ransomed. On the battlefield they are liberated. In the temple they are made pure. In the courtroom they are reprieved. In the slave market Jesus is the Ransom. On the battlefield he is the Victor. In the temple he is Priest and Lamb. In the courtroom he is the Condemned.

Metaphors apprehend rather than comprehend reality. Common figures of speech like raining cats and dogs or throwing out the baby with the bathwater or heart of gold ring true because they touch upon reality. All metaphors break down. That does not make them false but discloses the density of life and the limitations of language. Biblical metaphors are no exception. That said, metaphors testifying to the Crucified direct hearts and minds to deep realities like enslavement, oppression, impurity, and guilt. They invite us to God's mercy and justice experienced as freedom, victory, healing, and forgiveness. Testimony which engages imagination changes us. Testimony engages the way we think. But testimony also invites us to act. We are changed not simply by changing the way we think about or imagine God but foremost we are changed by our way of being in the world. Hearing the gospel of the crucified God requires living with the Crucified.

Recalling Jesus' last words, Paul persuades, "When we cry, 'Abba! Father!' it is that very Spirit bearing witness with our spirit that we are children of God, and if children, then heirs, heirs of God, and joint heirs with Christ—if, in fact, we suffer with him so that we may also be glorified with him" (Rom 8:15b–17). "Only the suffering God can help"—provided we suffer with him.

The gospel of the cross does not instantly resolve the problem of sin, evil, and suffering, nor does it sanction these systemic and personal powers

---

3. Guthrie, *Christian Doctrine*, 252–56.

by authorizing them as inevitable and invincible. The cross contradicts sin, evil, and suffering. The cross is God's *no* to sin, evil, and suffering. The cross defeats the disastrous consequences of our reaching and grasping and deception. The cross is God's word/act of forgiveness for sinners and the defeat of the powers which enslave them. The cross invites us to live by grace. But there is a reason Jesus enters the night alone. There is a reason we sleep as the disciples slept—we cannot save ourselves. While we cannot save ourselves we can, in view of the One praying in the garden alone, acknowledge our complicity and suffer with God by our love for the world which is made possible when we behold Jesus on the cross and not after we have taken him down.

COMPLICITY

Grace to you and peace from God our Father and the Lord Jesus Christ, who gave himself for our sins to set us free from the present evil age. —Gal 1:3–4

Sin, if there is such a thing, is somebody else's problem, not mine. I have no regrets. Ever heard that, ever felt that way? *Me, I don't need God's forgiveness. I'm getting along just fine, thank you. I'm already free. I don't worry about sin. It's my life and I'll live it how I please.* We are dodgy when it comes to complicity. Why is that? Moreover, why does God seemingly let us have our way? According to Paul, that is precisely what God does or so Paul tells his readers in Rome, "Claiming to be wise, they became fools; and they exchanged the glory of the immortal God for images resembling a mortal human being. . . . Therefore *God gave them up*" (Rom 1:22–24).

Giving up a child is every parent's worst nightmare. After trying everything humanly possible to spare and rescue children from their worst inclinations and predicaments, parents let go. Hosea may have had this nightmare in view when voicing God's turmoil over his recalcitrant people.

> When Israel was a child, I loved him and out of Egypt I called my son. The more I called them, the more they went from me. . . . Yet it was I who taught Ephraim to walk, I took them up in my arms; but they did not know that I healed them. I led them with cords of human kindness, with bands of love. I was to them like those who lift infants to their cheeks. . . . My people are bent on turning away from me. . . . How can I give you up. . . . How can I hand you over, O Israel? (Hos 11:1–8a)

In the end, Hosea concludes, God cannot. "My heart recoils within me; my compassion grows warm and tender. I will not execute my fierce anger. . . . I will not come in wrath" (Hos 11:8b-9).

Paul also correlates God's wrath with God giving us up to the consequences of our worst instincts. Only in Paul, God executes his wrath. God lets us have our way even when having our way brings harm. "Since they did not see fit to acknowledge God, *God gave them up* to a debased mind and to things that should not be done. They were filled with every kind of wickedness, evil, covetousness, malice. Full of envy, murder, strife, deceit, craftiness, they are gossips, slanderers, God-haters . . ." (Rom 1:28–32). God's wrath discloses our complicity and the awful consequences of our actions and inactions. As Moltmann observes, "guilt and punishment lie in one and the same event . . . [M]en who abandon God are abandoned by God. Godlessness and godforsakenness are two sides of the same event."[4]

Strangely, wrath also testifies to God's desire for our redemption. As Paul writes, "If God is for us, who is against us. He who did not withhold his own Son, but *gave him up* for all of us, will he not with him also give us everything else? (Rom 8:31–32). Though we are godless we are not godforsaken.[5] The Creator who is for us comes in wrath and is crucified as the godless and godforsaken One between thieves.

To understand why Jesus died requires that we speak in trinitarian terms. "The Son suffers dying, the Father suffers the death of the Son. The grief of the Father here is just as important as the death of the Son. The Fatherlessness of the Son is matched by the Sonlessness of the Father . . ."[6] Understanding the cross comes by meeting the One who bears the awful consequences of godlessness and godforsakenness. This meeting can only be described as fear-full because in this meeting we also face our complicity. "It is a fearful thing to fall into the hands of the living God" (Heb 10:31).

Ask yourself a few questions; some may even sound silly. Ever had a nice bacon cheeseburger and washed it down with your beverage of choice? Ever done that? Ever had a bottle of water? Ever flipped on a hundred-watt bulb? Ever traveled by car? How about by train or plane? Ever taken out trash? You know, the stuff that cannot be recycled, stuff we take to the curb that is picked up and buried who knows where when we are not looking. Ever taken out the trash? Are we complicit just by existing? Does our use of Earth's resources make us complicit—everything from the food we eat to the

---

4. Moltmann, *The Crucified God*, 242.
5. Moltmann, *The Crucified God*, 242.
6. Moltmann, *The Crucified God*, 243.

electricity that lights our space, everything that is grown, everything that is wasted and thrown away? Does that make us complicit?

Ask yourself another question. Which is more likely to happen: being killed by a terrorist or getting run over by a truck? If you answered *the truck*, you would be right. Globally, only 0.06 percent of all deaths result from terrorists. Road accidents account for about 2 percent. Car wrecks are a greater threat to life than terrorists, but where do we spend our money? In a typical fiscal year Americans spend six hundred times more on defense than transportation safety even though the odds and living proof indicate that wrecks are far more likely to kill us than terrorists. What are we really afraid of and what do our fears tell us?

Terrorism is no joking matter. Violent threat from terrorists and other enemies is horrible, despicable, indeed demonic, but are we not complicit as demonstrated by our willingness to fund arms and kill other humans in order to secure protection?

Examples of complicity could be multiplied many times over including personal ones like envy, strife, deceit, craftiness, gossip, slander, boasting, foolishness, heartlessness, and ruthlessness (Rom 1:29–31). Complicity ranges from private to corporate, from individual to social. It truly is our world—God's gift to us. How we tend and till it makes all of the difference. God invites us to choose life. A beginning, first step toward life comes by acknowledging our complicity. Denial is not the way forward. Blame is not the way forward. Dodging only compounds our distress. Nothing short of full-embodied confession brings life. The word for that is *repentance* ignited when we meet the *consuming fire* of the crucified God.

REDEMPTION

If any want to become my followers, let them deny themselves and take up their cross and follow me. —Matt 16:24

Jesus does not invite us to take up his cross, but our cross. There is an "infinite qualitative difference" between his cross and our cross. We do not take up the cross of Jesus, but our cross. Jesus takes up his cross to save us. We take up our cross to follow him. Suffering which accompanies contingent human existence is of a different order and will be addressed in chapter 11. Suffering which accompanies following Jesus occurs when we stand with the godless; when we welcome sojourners and stand with the alien. Suffering which helps occurs when we pursue reconciliation with those we deplore, when we love enemies. Following Jesus may and will bring failure, rejection, derision, and grave suspicion on exceptional occasions that we are forsaken. When we follow Jesus we may and will experience God forsakenness. We will suffer.

Jesus reserved his sharpest rebukes for disciples who craved religious and political power over others in order to avoid suffering. Remember what Jesus said to James and John who wanted to rule? Remember what he said when they argued about greatness? Remember what he said when they wanted to call down fire from heaven upon those who rejected Jesus? Remember the stinging rebuke Peter received when Jesus announced that he must undergo suffering and be rejected and killed? Peter took Jesus aside to set him straight. And what does Jesus do? He tells Peter, "Get behind me Satan! For you are setting your mind not on divine things but on human things" (Mark 8:31–33).

Jesus disappoints followers who desire power that orders social arrangements as the world orders them. His kingdom is not of this world. Jesus exercised power for the benefit of others. The rule of Jesus was not exploitative, destructive, or self-serving. His rule was self-emptying. Jesus looked to the interests of others, not his interests. His rule was humble, which should not be mistaken for cowardly, self-effacing hand-wringing. Jesus took up his cross and, like the suffering servant in Isaiah, set his face like flint. Jesus was determined to love the despised and rejected, the last, the least, the little, and the lost. We do no less when we refuse to take Jesus down from the cross and take up our cross and follow. And we can take up our cross because Jesus did not come down from his cross—God *gave him up* for the salvation of the world.

In the next chapter we will explore how this Christ-shaped life of resolute love is lived in hope as we turn our thoughts to consider why Jesus was raised from the dead.

Chapter 8

Why Was Jesus Raised From The Dead?

IDLE TALE OR GOSPEL?

But these words seemed to them an idle tale, and they did not believe them. —Luke 24:11

God raised Jesus from the dead to change the world, to change us, to change you. God raised Jesus from the dead to make you, to make us, to make the world, new. The godless and godforsaken One who was crucified in weakness and folly has been raised in power and wisdom and now rules. Jesus is Lord.

Just as we do not know Jesus apart from taking up our cross, so we do not know the risen Christ apart from living into the new life his resurrection brings. Jesus was raised from the dead not by our faith, but by the One "who gives life to the dead and calls into existence the things that do not exist" (Rom 4:17). Hope is not something we give ourselves; it is the gift of God who raised the godless and godforsaken One. That kind of hope is hard to come by and harder still to live. Just as we try to "take Jesus down from the cross" to make God accessible, reachable, and comprehensible, so we try to "raise him up." The consequence is something less than living hope. Before saying what hope is, I want to say what hope is not.

The resurrection of Jesus is not simply *an event* that happened long ago. When the resurrection of Jesus is reduced to a long ago event it becomes an ossified doctrine. Echoes of this may be overheard in language like accepting or letting or making Jesus our personal Lord when or because we believe God raised him from the dead. We do not make Jesus Lord. Jesus is Lord because God raised the Crucified and exalted him to his right hand.

Secondly, the resurrection of Jesus is not simply a wish, a prospect, or *an idea*, which, like an inevitable spring, happens when people engage in betterment projects or forgive one another or act in other ways that are consistent with the moral vision of Jesus as expressed, for example, in the Sermon on the Mount. Echoes of this may be overheard in language such as building or spreading or bringing in the kingdom of God. Jesus is Lord separate and apart from us spreading and building or bringing in his kingdom. Peter, testifying to the gift of the Holy Spirit presently at work, put it this way, "This Jesus God raised up, and of that all of us are witnesses. Being therefore exalted at the right hand of God, and having received from the Father the promise of the Holy Spirit, he has poured out this that you both see and hear" (Acts 2:32). If we spread, build, or bring in the kingdom, we do so only because Jesus already is Lord. Good news is hard to hear and harder still to live as hope.

Consider the responses of those who first heard news about the risen Christ. And remember they were not camped in the graveyard waiting for Jesus to spring from the tomb. The disciples hid behind closed doors, locked away in the city. When these frightened souls heard news of Easter they dismissed it as an idle tale. Some went to the tomb and saw that it was empty. They fled "for terror and amazement had seized them; and they said nothing to anyone, for they were afraid" (Mark 16:8).

We should go easy on the disciples. Crucified rabbis are supposed to remain dead. In our more honest moments, we may find ourselves identifying not only with those who hid or dismissed or fled but also with two disciples on the Emmaus Road who met but did not recognize the risen Lord. Standing still and looking sad they told the unrecognized risen One, "We had hoped that he was the one to redeem Israel" (Luke 24:21). Hope which is living good news and not talismanic doctrine or mytheme optimism comes by grace through faith (Eph 2:8).

Seventy years ago Bonhoeffer observed that we have learned in all things to get along without recourse to "the working hypothesis of God."[1] Yes, of course, people still believe in God and Christians still worship. The principalities and powers are happy to concede an hour on Sunday mornings. What harm can come from a few prayers and hymns? And yes, give Christians their due on some voter value issues. We will toss in a few laws regarding personal morality knowing full-well who is in charge of weightier

---

1. Bonhoeffer, *Letters & Papers from Prison*, 360.

matters and it is not Jesus. We will even invite the preacher to bless kick-offs—even the opening of Congress itself.

Silicon Valley, Wall Street, big energy, and their global counterparts pay good money to run this world. The Capitol Rotunda, the Kremlin, the Palace of Westminster, the Great Hall of the People are open for business. Mastery over Earth through politics, science and technology, social media, and religion may bring progress but not living hope. Living hope comes by following the living Lord.

THE CRUCIFIED IS RISEN

Why are you frightened, and why do doubts arise in your hearts? Look at my hands and my feet; see that it is I myself. —Luke 24:38

The gospel is not testimony about a dead man brought to life, but testimony about the godless and godforsaken Jewish rabbi, Jesus, who was crucified and raised from the dead. The gospel is not an idea about immortality or eternal life or an impersonal force unleashed in the universe which inevitably trends toward justice and mercy. The gospel is God's victory over sin, evil, suffering, and death won in Jesus who was crucified and raised from the dead by God's act of new creation.

The crisis of the Anthropocene is fueled by the notion that history has no purpose, no goal, or narrative aside and apart from what we give it. The crisis of the Anthropocene is that we are stuck in the *closed circle of our humanity* and as a consequence we are as good as dead.[2] Through the death of Jesus, God descends into the realm of the dead or as the Apostles' Creed puts it, he descends into hell.[3] Or, as Paul exclaimed, "nothing can ever separate us from the love of God in Christ Jesus our Lord . . ." (Rom 8:39). Nothing, not even nihilism, can separate us from God.

In the epoch of the Anthropocene, nihilism poses our greatest threat. Of course, you would not know it by the smiling happy faces of the sanguine and well-fed. Furrowed brows crease a brooding few and cynics abound, but the official creed of the Anthropocene is sunny mastery measured by economic progress. The official creed of the Anthropocene is represented by Prometheus though in some dark corner of our soul we suspect that the real representative is Sisyphus.[4]

---

2. Barth, *The Epistle to the Romans*, 253.
3. Presbyterian Church (U.S.A.), *Book of Confessions*, 21.
4. Moltmann, *Theology of Hope*, 24.

The word of the cross breaks the deadening powers represented by Sisyphus and Prometheus. While defeated, they remain powerful. God's verdict through the resurrection of the Crucified has been rendered, but a battle remains to be waged by those who live in hope.

CONTRADICTION

Faith is the assurance of things hoped for, the conviction of things not seen. —Heb 11:1

Jesus was crucified in public. The risen Lord appeared only to disciples. The death of Jesus is open to historical investigation. Resurrection does not fall into the same category. Sources other than the Bible confirm that a Jewish rabbi named Jesus from Nazareth, charged as a zealot and blasphemer, was crucified under the reign of Pontius Pilate. That historical reality is beyond dispute. Resurrection, on the other hand, is not observable. It is not accessible to historical observation. God is not an object in the universe alongside other objects that may be observed. The resurrection of the Crucified was not and cannot be observed. The Bible is silent regarding what happened in the tomb. No one witnessed the resurrection. The risen One appears only to followers, not to Pilate, not to Caiaphas, not to any neutral observers.

Jesus appeared only to followers. As Paul put it, "even though we once knew Christ from a human point of view, we know him no longer in that way" (2 Cor 5:17). Acknowledging this does not throw us back on ourselves as if faith raises Jesus from the dead. The acknowledgement throws us ever more fully into the arms of God. God reveals God through God and the means God chooses. And God reveals himself to the godless and godforsaken. God's revelation is grace, not nostalgia, not utopia, but promise: "I will be with you always, to the end of the age" (Matt 28:20).

Followers of the crucified but risen Lord live in but not of the world. Followers are strangers and aliens in the world because followers dare to hope that they live in the twilight of sin, evil, suffering, and death. Followers are wide awake. They see the world as it is and it is not yet "very good." Followers live with the contradiction between what is and what will be, which does not produce enmity with the world, but passionate resistance to the status quo established and maintained by the principalities and powers—pretenders to the rule of God. Resistance is not grim determination, but joyful fighting for the world knowing the victory won through the Crucified who has been raised from the dead.

Followers answer the crushing noise of Anthropocene nihilism with the resounding symphony of hope through Jesus Christ. Followers live with the givenness of things in tension with the givenness of things as they shall be, a givenness seen in advance through Christ risen. Followers do not live with their heads in the air, but with their boots on the ground. Followers acknowledge that things are not as they are supposed to be and live into the future that shall be. Followers live in hope.

DAWN HORIZON

After the Sabbath, as the first day of the week was dawning, Mary Magdalene and the other Mary went to see the tomb. —Matt 28:1

The sun does not cast any shadows at noon. What about as day stretches toward night and the "shadows lengthen and the busy world is hushed, and the fever of life is over, and our work is done?"[5] Does day follow night? Was the psalmist wishfully thinking when he wrote that "even the darkness is not dark to you; the night is as bright as the day, for darkness is as light to you" (Ps 139:12). Does day follow night? Does day break?

Think about that word—*break*. Tree limbs break. Arms break. Levees break. Damns break. Glass is broken in emergencies. *Break* sounds violent as captured by its synonym, *crack*. Breaking is forceful. But dawn breaking—that sounds, well, it sounds benign, non-threatening, beautiful even. Daybreaks can be and are beautiful but they are also disruptive. Day breaking shakes us or may shake us out of sleeping complacency. Day breaking may crack us wide awake. Dawn breaking makes us more fully alive and attuned so that we not only see the world as it is with all of its shadows but as it shall be in the full light of noon day. Hope springs from the dawn horizon of Easter. Drawn by that Light we are awakened and newly made.

There is a fascinating image in that very odd and last book of the Bible—Revelation. It reads, "I saw no temple in the city, for its temple is the Lord God the Almighty and the Lamb. And the city has no need of sun or moon to shine on it, for the glory of God is its light, and its lamp is the Lamb. The nations will walk by its light, and the kings of the earth will bring their glory into it. Its gates will never be shut by day—and there will be *no night* there" (Rev 21:22–25). Jesus says no one knows, not even he knows, when that day will be. Here and now, because night is broken we anticipate that day because of Easter's first light. The Crucified has been raised.

---

5. Presbyterian Church (U.S.A.), *Book of Common Worship*, 228.

We do not individually or collectively bring the Day of the Lord, no more so than any one of us or all of us together cause the sun to rise. But we do walk toward that Day. We live by God's promise walking toward the Light. We walk because Christ is the Light. The great achievement and failure of the progressive movement was the mistaken notion that we can, by our labor and faith or some combination of the two, bring in the full light of God's day. The progressive project, a vestige of Christendom, was matched by the great achievement and failure of evangelicalism which anticipated God's day by winning the world for Christ one soul at a time. Christ will win the world but it will not be because there are churches on every corner of Earth's farthest reaches. In the city of God, there is no temple—no church. "The temple is the Lord God the Almighty and the Lamb" (Rev 21:22).

If not progressivism or evangelicalism—what then? Perhaps, and this is a big perhaps, we should live into the promise of God without defining the form of things to come. Bonhoeffer expressed this imagined future as *religionless Christianity*.[6] Bonhoeffer imagined that institutional expressions of Christianity should not be mistaken for Christ. Writing from his Tegel prison, he suggested to a friend, "To be a Christian does not mean to be religious in a particular way . . . but to be a man—not a type of man, but the man that Christ creates in us. It is not the religious act that makes the Christian, but participation in the sufferings of God in secular life."[7] Bonhoeffer insisted that we should live realizing that all things earthly, including institutional expressions of Christian faith, are *pen-ultimate* (his word) or provisional. And yet, as Bonhoeffer also warned and testified, salvation does not mean *extrication*. Salvation is better defined as contradiction.

Contradiction means that we live, as Luther said, as saints and sinners. We are not one or the other but both at once. We live in but not of the world. We do not live out of the world or above the world but in the world, not like the world but contrary to it—contrary to the claims made on us by its principalities and powers. We live contrary to what is, which means we push back, resist, and oppose things as they are.

Jesus was not crucified because he was a poet-philosopher. Jesus made governing authorities mad because he contradicted their rule. He threatened their arrangements of social, political, and religious power. Frightened by his opposition, they killed him. Resurrection is not simply vindication that Jesus was right to push back, it is that but more. Resurrection is God's way in the world—giving life to the dead and calling into existence the things that do not exist.

---

6. Bonhoeffer, *Letters & Papers from Prison*, 280–82.

7. Bonhoeffer, *Letters & Papers from Prison*, 361.

Christian hope is not first the work of reform or revival or retrieval or revolution. Christian hope is new creation predicated upon the Crucified whom God raised. We do not let or make this One Lord—Jesus is the Lord and has been and will be until that Day when God will be "all in all" (1 Cor 15:28), a theme for chapter 20.

The stance of followers here and now is always provisional, always fragmentary and is so because it is always open to what God is doing and will do. Living hope does not extricate us from the present situation of the Anthropocene; hope empowers us to contradict the claims and trajectory of the Anthropocene. That does not make us misanthropes. With the godless and godforsaken One, we are philanthropes. We are for fellow human beings. We love our home—Earth. "God so loved the world . . ." (John 3:16–17). That love breaks forth in hope for the world as it shall be beginning when we awake and live in the Light. Contours of this hope will be traced in the next chapter, "What Does God Want From Us?"

Chapter 9

What Does God Want From Us?

COUNTING OUR DAYS

So teach us to count our days that we may gain a wise heart. —Ps 90:12

What does God want from us? Asked another way, how do we count our days? In this chapter you are invited to count your days prompted by a confession of faith: the God who creates redeems and the God who redeems creates.

One day I was speaking with my daughter when our phone conversation was interrupted by a budding new talker. My granddaughter, Cora, then two months shy of her second birthday, was into something or demanded something from her mother. Laughing out loud my daughter said that Cora had discovered the ubiquitous and occasionally offending first-person objective case possessive pronoun *me*. Every parent of a two-year-old knows something about the trying and wonderful discovery of that pronoun. In great measure our humanness is announced by this two-letter pronoun.

Me is such a tiny word, but what a difference it makes. *Me* expresses the human capacity to recognize *not-me*. We are nature but we are not completely bound by nature. As my two-year-old granddaughter is discovering, you and I transcend nature. Soon enough Cora's transcendence of nature will be aided by other masteries such as turning on lights, adjusting thermostats, and one day reading books or perhaps solving algebraic equations. Like all other humans, Cora is part of nature but she is not entirely bound by it. Her unboundedness—acknowledged or not, conscious or not—is expressed by requests for water or her mother's attention, sometimes made with a cry but mostly smiles. Cora is bound to nature but not in the same way a tree is bound.

A tree cannot request water or walk to water or dig a well. It may extend its roots and over time a species may adapt and given enough time and luck it may even become a different tree, a new species that survives or fits a more arid climate. Humans also adapt, which perhaps drives self-transcendence. Walk for a day without water and we are compromised. Add several more days and we are near death. We transcend nature but we are also bound by nature.

Self-transcendence makes humans unique among Earth's creatures. It also makes us uniquely vulnerable. Our complex mastery has woven a gossamer web of life which creates enormous possibilities but also peril. Mastery sets us apart from nature, but not entirely. Indeed, mastery creates the illusion that we are boundless when in fact we depend on Earth.

My grandchildren expect apples year-round. When I was a child, apples were a fall treat. They could be preserved and enjoyed during winter months but freshly picked fruit was available only in season. Today, thanks to a fossil-fueled supply chain, fresh apples may be eaten year-round. Mastery gives us year-round fresh apples, but not without consequence. How long would we last if the food supply chain failed entirely, not just apples but everything?

If the last two hundred years and the past seventy in particular teach nothing else, they announce that our lives are bound to Earth. Whether or not we listen remains to be seen, but the announcement has been made. Failure to listen may bring our demise. Earth will abide. Earth will continue without us. It did with five previous extinctions. Earth may be indifferent to us but our indifference imperils our existence. It behooves us to listen and "to count our days that we may gain a wise heart."

Historians "count" days and we are all historians with or without framed parchment. We number our days. We assign names to them—all 4.5 billion years and counting. The most recent ones we named Holocene from two Greek words meaning *entire* and *recent* or *entirely recent*, which, as noted earlier, began some twelve thousand years ago with a warm spell. The scientific debate over whether or not we have entered a new epoch known as the Anthropocene or *recent human* continues. (For an excellent review of the science and history of the term and debates about it, see *The Human Planet: How We Created the Anthropocene*, written by Simon Lewis and Mark Maslin). While scientific study and debate continue, all people, whether of faith or no faith or uncertain faith, can ill afford to regard Earth as a disposable stage which may be despoiled, wasted, and tossed aside when the curtain is drawn. Among some Christians, echoes of this are commonly expressed as escaping Earth when Jesus returns by being "caught up in the clouds" while unfortunate others are left behind (1 Thess 4:17).

The sweeping narrative of the Bible, including our death and being "at home with the Lord," does not promote escape but completion of God's purposes. The last book of the Bible expressed this with the symbol of "a new heaven and a new earth" (Rev 21:1). Paul captured a like faith when he wrote, "We know that the whole creation has been groaning in labor pains until now; and not only the creation, but we ourselves, who have the first fruits of the Spirit, groan inwardly while we wait for adoption, the redemption of our bodies" (Rom 8:22–23). Humans and creation will be redeemed.

I will return to this theme in greater detail in chapter 20. Here I want to emphasize that Christian faith is decidedly worldly, made more so by the day that has dawned with the resurrection of the Crucified. Those who follow the Risen One live expectantly anticipating that day. We live in hope here and now because we have hope for the hereafter. It does not yet appear what we shall be. We live in this not-yet hour anticipating the future that we have witnessed in the Crucified who is risen. Dawn breaks when the hereafter invades and contradicts the here and now. It does so when we heed the commands to love God and our neighbors and when we love Earth.

TWO COMMANDS

Jesus answered, "The first commandment is, 'Hear O Israel: the Lord our God, the Lord is one; you shall love the Lord your God with all your heart, and with all your soul, and with all of your mind, and with all your strength.' The second is this, 'You shall love your neighbor as yourself.' There is no other commandment greater than these."
—Mark 12:29–31

The title of this chapter suggests that God wants something, that God desires something of us, which may seem like a conceit, but such is the nature of God—God desires or wants communion with creation, not out of need but from sheer delight, a joy reflected in the first observation God makes of creation: "It is not good that the man should be alone." (Gen 2:18). How curious that this is the first judgment rendered by God. What would God know of aloneness? Then again, if God is relationship, which trinitarian theology insists, and if we are made in the image of God, then God's verdict of "not good" means that we are human only in relationship and not in solitude or isolation.

Late in the New Testament John writes, "Those who do not love a brother or sister whom they have seen, cannot love God whom they have not seen" (1 John 4:20). Consider how John makes this claim, "The commandment we have from him is this: those who love God must love their brothers and sisters also" (1 John 4:21). We love others, John persuades, because we love God. But here is a greater curiosity and mystery: "We love because he first loved us" (1 John 4:19).

Our love for others overflows from the inexhaustible love of God. Our love does not result from the force of a brute command. Love derives from God's desire for communion. God does not command what God does not provide. God, who gives life to the dead and calls into existence things that are not, generates love—our love for God and our love for others. Love born of God is earthly-minded. It is incarnate and when the situation demands, it is sacrificial. In all of its varied expressions, love is generated by God's vulnerable and bountiful delight in creation.

PEOPLE OF THE DAY

What does the LORD require of you but to do justice, and to love kindness, and to walk humbly with your God? —Mic 6:8

God's generative love makes all things new. As with the first covenant, so with the second covenant, God's generative love creates a community. Followers of Jesus Christ are called out of aloneness and death into community and life. Those enslaved to sin are freed to walk as in the day. We live here and now fully alive to the world as it shall be. We live in hope disclosed in the crucified but risen Christ who is coming and who now rules. This life is not utopian or revolutionary but reflective and generative of the world that shall be. Followers are active recipients. God's love newly makes and sends us to be salt and light and leaven. While hidden and small we are "more than conquerors through him who loved us" (Rom 8:37).

Through Christ's resurrection God generates a new community and new possibilities. The unjust are justified to do justice. The unjust are freed from retaliation and collapse to practice forgiveness which gives birth to flourishing. The guilty are freed from shame to show mercy. Those laid low are raised up to walk humbly. The once worthless are now worthy. Resurrection faith does not anesthetize followers to suffering but awakens followers to shoulder suffering, a burden made lighter because their yoke is shared by the Risen One. Christians are saved from ungodliness and god forsakenness. And they are saved to godliness and God-with-us-ness. Deliverance breaks and heals the tragic and harmful consequences of sin by sending us newly made to love the world. Our way in the world is the way of Jesus Christ.

CONTRADICTION AS NON-CONFORMITY

I appeal to you therefore, brothers and sisters, by the mercies of God, to present your bodies as a living sacrifice, holy and acceptable to God, which is your spiritual worship. Do not be conformed to this world, but be transformed by the renewing of your minds, so that you may discern what is the will of God—what is good and acceptable and perfect. —Rom 12:1–2

If nihilism is the greatest threat in the epoch of the Anthropocene, hope is not just its anodyne but finally its antidote. With the resurrection of the Crucified, day has broken. Like Moses on Pisgah who saw the promised land from a distance, so we behold the risen Christ on the horizon. In this next-to-the-last world, beholding is partial but it is nonetheless true and sufficient beholding. Referring to "the light of the knowledge of the glory of God in the face of Jesus Christ," Paul concludes that we "have this treasure in clay jars so that it may be clear that this extraordinary power belongs to God and does not come from us" (2 Cor 4:6–7). Like John, Paul understood that God generates not only our love but also our beholding of God's light. Jesus invites us to let that light shine, to put it on a bushel basket so that all in the house may see and give glory to God (Matt 5:14–16).

Our *no* to nihilism results in more than scolding condemnation. Our *no* to nihilism is heard only alongside others, in solidarity with others through self-emptying humility, a resolute, proud humility. Our way in the world, no less than our Savior's, will be marked by conflict, contention, controversy, contest, and contradiction. The strange consolation of hope in the Crucified is not mournful, despairing consolation, much less self-pitying.[1] Resurrection stands us on our feet marching us toward God's new creation, not timidly but assuredly, confident that our Redeemer lives. We are not removed from sorrow or suffering but transformed in times of sorrow and suffering. We grieve but not as those without hope (1 Thess 4:13). Hope sends us ready to engage the world by greeting every day as the first day.

---

1. Moltmann, *The Way of Jesus Christ*, 193.

Hope is expressed in three realms: economic, political, and religious. Matthew and Luke refer to these three realms in the temptation of Jesus. I will follow Luke's order.

The Synoptic Gospels frame the temptation of Jesus within the broader work of the Spirit. In Mark, after his baptism by John, Jesus is *driven* into the wilderness. In Matthew and Luke Jesus is *led* to the scene. This difference aside, all three frame the temptation of Jesus within the purpose of God or what God wants from us.

The first temptation is economic. A famished Jesus is invited to turn stone into bread. He answers that humans do not live by bread alone. Jesus will feed the hungry and encourages his disciples to do the same. Jesus eats with the hungry and encourages table fellowship among his followers. Jesus so identifies with the hungry that he announces to his followers that whenever they feed the hungry they feed him (Matt 25:35). Hope contradicts those forces which deny bread to the hungry but hope is not exhausted in bread alone. Humans are created for communion with God.

In the second temptation, the devil led Jesus up and showed him all the kingdoms of the world. He offered Jesus power over every kingdom in exchange for one thing: worship me and it will all be yours (Luke 4:6). How convenient if all problems could be resolved by political solutions. The trade-off is that while promising freedom, the state enslaves those who give it sole allegiance. Followers of Christ live as salt and light and leaven remembering that the state crucified the Savior. Followers have one Sovereign, the Creator who redeems and now rules.

Perhaps Luke saved religion for last to suggest that religion remains the greatest temptation. Why wouldn't Jesus "throw" himself down from the "pinnacle of the temple" and prove once and for all his true identity? Would that not have convinced everyone of the reality of God? Luke returns to this temptation on Golgotha when not once but three times Jesus is enticed to save himself by coming down from the cross—a mighty act of self-preservation asserted to convince a doubting, despairing, and hopeless world. Jesus declines.

The way of Jesus is the way of the cross. It is also the way of those who would follow. This way does not extricate us from the world by making us big and powerful and noticed, most especially in cathedrals of spectacle. Our way is hidden. It is the way of the cross. It is also the way of resurrection. We are born into "a living hope" (1 Pet 1:3). That is what God wants from us: to live in hope. In the next chapter we will trace a trajectory of this living hope and how it may be heard and embodied among a multitude of nations.

Chapter 10

A Chosen Few Or A Multitude Of Nations?

GOD'S DESIRE

This is right and acceptable in the sight of God our Savior, who desires everyone to be saved and to come to the knowledge of the truth. —1Tim 2:3-4

God "desires everyone to be saved." Are there exceptions? May God's desire be resisted and finally denied? Will a chosen few be saved or a multitude? To prompt imagination I will first offer brief reflections on the character of God's desire and call along with considerations of our response and commission.

God, who is love, creates from love, for love, to love which never ends. Like beauty, God's love is the means and the end of God's desire. How can any refuse God's love? Or, as Paul once asked, "[W]ho can resist his will?" (Rom 9:19). That is a great mystery—the presence of "not good." Creation, including humankind, does not always and everywhere reflect God's desire. The presence of "not good" under the rubric of suffering will occupy the next chapter. Here my concern specifically regards the "not good" of refusing communion with God, the "not good" of living separate and estranged from God, indifferent, and even hostile to God. How can anyone refuse God's love? Asked differently, how is it that anyone knows that they are created from God's love, for love, to God's love which never ends? In brief, we know by hearing the word of the Crucified whom God raised from the dead. The communion God desires God creates through faith. By grace through faith, we become partners in God's new creation, but I am getting ahead of myself. How do we hear this word of welcome which makes us and is making all things new? How do we hear good news?

God makes and keeps promises. God also anticipates a response from us, but God is not a deal-maker. Hearing the gospel is not a transaction. I am aware of the if-then language found in the Bible expressed in texts like Deut 30:15–16.

> See, I have set before you today life and prosperity, death and adversity. If you obey the commandments of the LORD your God that I am commanding you today, by loving the LORD your God, walking in his ways, and observing his commandments, decrees, and ordinances, then you shall live and become numerous, and the LORD your God will bless you in the land that you are entering to possess.

I am also aware that first covenant language is echoed by second covenant language such as, "[I]f you confess with your lips that Jesus is Lord and believe in your heart that God raised him from the dead, then you will be saved" (Rom 10:9). God creates and respects human agency. Conditions also accompany God's covenant; but, in keeping with Scripture, we must also confess that humans are not commodities. God desires communion. And communion is not a deal. It is a relationship. Communion, alternately rendered *with union* or *together one*, expresses God's desired communion with all humans, a desire declared through the spoken and written word and the Word made flesh.

Communion with God is asymmetrical. God is great—we are small. God is good—we are not so-good. God is eternal—we are transient. This and more reflects the asymmetry of communion with God. So, how does God save us and not enslave us? How does God help us without making us helpless? Asymmetry too often results or is expressed in patron-client terms. In some expressions of Christian faith, God's otherness overwhelms our humanity, making us invisible and uninvolved. God does not smother us with love. Equally so, God is not simply an advisor, whisperer, or validator of what and who we already are. God is the Victor but the victory makes us more than former victims. God is the Liberator but we are more than released captives. God is the Redeemer but we are more than purchased slaves. Communion with God is asymmetrical but such that we become more fully who we were created to be—not less. By grace through faith God stands us on our feet enabling us to resist, overcome, and reform the "not good" which separates us from God. Communion with God is made possible by God's call.

CALL

As Jesus was walking along, he saw a man called Matthew sitting at the tax booth; and he said to him, "Follow me." And he got up and followed him. —Matt 9:9

How did Matthew get up from his tax booth and follow? How do any of us ever get up? We get up and follow by the grace of God's call. The asymmetry of God's call and our response is reflected in Luke 4:14-30. According to Luke, Jesus made his first public utterance in Nazareth on a Sabbath. Jesus was given "the scroll of the prophet Isaiah" and read these words, "The Spirit of the Lord is upon me, because he has anointed me to bring good news to the poor. He has sent me to proclaim release to the captives and recovery of sight to the blind, to let the oppressed go free, to proclaim the year of the Lord's favor." Jesus rolled up the scroll, returned it to the attendant, and sat down. With every eye in his hometown synagogue fixed on him, Jesus said, "Today this scripture has been fulfilled in your hearing."

The audacity of the announcement was not lost on his listeners who first praised Jesus for his gracious words but then wondered aloud about his paternity, "Is not this Joseph's son?" Affirmation turned to alarm and then to mob action when Jesus reminded his listeners of God's grace in former times toward a Syrian outsider identified as Naaman. The mob drove Jesus out of town and onto a hilltop, which would have been the end of him had Jesus not "passed though the midst of them and went on his way." Hearing good news of God's liberation may and often does greet insiders as bad news, especially when it includes good news for outsiders. But such is hearing the gospel. We "get up" when God's call breaks settled patterns of inclusion and exclusion. We "get up" when we hear God's call which extends mercy to all.

Paul, a contemporary of Luke, also testified that "faith comes from what is heard" adding that "what is heard comes through the word of Christ" (Rom 10:17). Translators don't agree: Did Paul mean the word *about* Christ or the word *from* Christ. Translation aside, the intent is clear: faith comes from hearing about or from Christ who is not dead and gone, a figure frozen in the past, but alive and present. Hearing is possible not only because God has spoken but also because God continues to speak and will speak again. Paul witnessed to this present living Word when he reasons that "no one can say 'Jesus is Lord' except by the Holy Spirit" (1 Cor 12:3). Hearing God's call is a work of the Spirit.

Nowhere does Paul more categorically express the asymmetry of communion with God than in his nuanced testimony found in Romans 9:1—11:36. Paul declares that God's desire to extend mercy "depends not on human will or exertion, but on God . . ." God loves those whom God chooses without first consulting us and securing our approval.

Paul is not alone in the radical priority given to God's gracious calling. John's Gospel conveys a like conviction with the well-rehearsed story of Nicodemus who comes to Jesus by night (John 3:1–21). Nicodemus, an esteemed leader of establishment Judaism, is curious about Jesus. Calling Jesus *Rabbi*, Nicodemus observes that no one could do what Jesus had done "apart from the presence of God." Jesus responded to the curious seeker in these now famous words, "Very truly, I tell you, no one can see the kingdom of God without being born from above." The impossibility is not lost on Nicodemus who states the absurd, "Can one enter a second time into the mother's womb and be born?"

The Rabbi and the Pharisee are miscommunicating. Jesus insists that he is not speaking in riddles, but in a tradition known to Nicodemus. "The wind blows where it chooses, and you hear the sound of it, but you do not know where it comes from or where it goes. So it is with everyone who is born of the Spirit." Faith is not something we give ourselves nor is it something we can give to another. Faith is not inherited. Faith transcends genes, ethnicity, nationality, social class, gender, and other markers of human distinction or as 1 John says, "Everyone who believes that Jesus is the Christ has been born of God" (1 John 5:1). Christians may be baptized in a cathedral or down by a river. They may be confirmed before high altars or converted through the internet. By whatever instrument, the Spirit, like wind, is free, hidden, and beyond human control or manipulation.

The Spirit's calling is not limited by place or circumstance. Matthew was at his tax booth. James and John were mending their nets. The woman of the city was cowed by a mob. The Samaritan woman was drawing water from a well. Zacchaeus was perched in a tree. All heard the Spirit calling. Calling is not restricted to high church altars, prestigious pulpits, or to any other means. God publishes God's desire by the means of his choosing.

RESPONSE

The next day Jesus decided to go to Galilee. He found Philip and said to him, "Follow me." Now Philip was from Bethsaida, the city of Andrew and Peter. Philip found Nathanael and said to him, "We have found him about whom Moses in the law and also the prophets wrote, Jesus son of Joseph from Nazareth." Nathanael said to him, "Can anything good come out of Nazareth?" Philip said to him, "Come and see." —John 1:43–46

If the central confession of the first covenant is expressed by, "The LORD is our God, the LORD alone" (Deut 6:4); the driving confession of the second covenant is, "Jesus is Lord" (1 Cor 12:3). If professing faith in Jesus as Lord is central, what did Jesus mean when he concluded the Sermon on the Mount with these sobering, shocking words, "Not everyone who says to me, 'Lord, Lord,' will enter the kingdom of God, but only the one who does the will of my Father in heaven" (Matt 7:21). Is grace really free or does it come with a price? God loves you, maybe? God loves you, if? Is God a deal maker after all: an offer is laid on the table, the terms and conditions of which apply only upon signing? Is that how it works? Salvation is conditional, contingent, and finally dependent on our response? God loves us, maybe? God loves us when . . . ?

A beginning answer may be found by naming two parodies of faith. These were not unknown in the first century and they are not unknown today. The two may be represented by the magician-client relationship and the relationship between spectacle and spectators.

Clients believe magicians possess unique powers which are available for clients' needs but only when certain conditions are met. By clicking her heels and repeating three times that "there's no place like home," Dorothy may return to Kansas or so the wizard promised. Magical thinking is silly. But is Dorothy any sillier than drivers who think that they will be young or attractive or vivacious by purchasing an expensive SUV capable of scaling a forty-five degree stepped incline on a Chinese mountaintop? Magical thinking was not left behind when we entered the *modern* era any more than spectacle ended when Rome abolished gladiator games in the fifth century. One example: spectacle continues on Friday nights and on a day once called the Lord's Day when spectators get the thrill of victory and the agony of defeat without blood, sweat, or tears excepting groceries for tailgating, the price of admission, or Monday morning disputes about how things would have turned out differently had they been coaching or playing on the field. Spectators can be fanatic.

Is it too far of a stretch to imagine Christian faith as spectacle or magic, neither of which expects nor demands anything yet with all of the benefits? You know, we go to the show for baptisms, confirmations, (or revivals, take your pick), weddings, funerals, and those not to be missed beard and bathrobe Christmas pageants and truly majestic Easter spectacles, but not much else in between. And by the way, doesn't it just give you goose bumps when the choir sings the *Hallelujah Chorus*? Makes you want to stand and cheer.

Is it any wonder Christian faith gets a bad name? It gets the name Christians give it. And when witness looks like magic and acts like spectacle what should we expect? The problem is not Jesus.

Faith comes by hearing, listening, and obeying Jesus. When we remove the stigma of the cross by living in conformity to the world or eliminate sacrifice expressed in the ethic of the Sermon on the Mount, we depart from Jesus. Faith comes when we take up our cross and abide with Christ. That is not a deal but a lifelong relationship where we participate bodily and spiritually in God's new creation. Grace is received through faithful response.

COMMISSIONING

Jesus came and said to them, "All authority in heaven and on earth has been given to me. Go therefore and make disciples of all nations, baptizing them in the name of the Father, and of the Son and of the Holy Spirit, and teaching them to obey everything that I have commanded you. And remember, I am with you always, to the end of the age." —Matt 28:18–20

Some weeks before Jesus commissioned his disciples a man described as young and wealthy approached Jesus and asked what he needed to do to have eternal life (Matt 19:16–30). Jesus told him to keep the commandments. The young man said he had; was there anything else? Jesus said, "Sell your possessions, and give the money to the poor . . . and follow me." The story ends on a depressing note. The young man "went away grieving for he had many possessions." Actually, the story did not end there. When the young man walked away Jesus turned to his disciples and told them that it is hard for rich people to enter the kingdom. Camels, Jesus said, have an easier time passing through the eye of a needle than rich people have entering the kingdom. The disciples were "astounded." Disturbed, they ask, "Then who can be saved?" Jesus looked at them and said, "For mortals it is impossible, but for God all things are possible."

Followers of Christ are commissioned by God who makes all things possible. They are sent to bear witness in word and deed to what they have seen and heard in Jesus Christ. Results belong to God. How many will be saved—a chosen few or a vast multitude—Christians only or people from north and south, east and west? Rather than worrying about the number, which none of us is asked to do anyway, God calls us to listen, hear, obey, follow, and make disciples. Our lived response to grace, our communion with God, announces God's desire. Results and judgment belong to God. We make disciples when we follow. We make disciples when we invite others to "come and see" (John 1:35–51). It is not magic and it is not spectacle. Salvation comes by grace through faith.

Invitations to grace come through relationships, friends inviting friends and friends welcoming strangers to "come and see." Salvation comes by grace through many faithful relationships and not simply by a few charismatic evangelists, elite clergy, clever church growth programs, or sophisticated, well-funded mission strategies. Results rest the shoulders of another. Judgment belongs to God who "desires everyone to be saved." All things are possible with God—the salvation of a vast multitude. The number is not for us to say. Our hope resides in God who desires all to be saved. And salvation "depends not on human will or exertion, but on God who shows mercy." We are called by the Spirit to embody good news in living testimony. We are called to hope for all nations and people.

In the next chapter we will consider, why suffering? Why is creation not always and everywhere "very good?"

Chapter 11

Why Suffering?

IMPERFECTION

My God, My God, why have you forsaken me? Why are you so far from helping me, from the words of my groaning? O my God, I cry by day, but you do not answer; by night, but find no rest. . . . Dominion belongs to the LORD, he rules over the nations. —Ps 22:1–2, 28

The psalmist's cry of godforsaken-ness no less than his confession that God rules all nations is a cry of faith. Faith does not explain suffering but seeks to understand God. Faith, which anticipates deliverance, is embodied through lament, protest, and works of healing in a world which is "very good" but fraught with "not good." We live between God's promised redemption and its completion. In this chapter, I do not intend to explain suffering. My aim is to testify to hope in the face of suffering.

Humans did not suddenly discover the problem of suffering with the dawn of the Enlightenment, but the question was reframed by that age—reason displaced faith and after Descartes (1596–1650) increasingly drove theological conversation. This chapter will follow the advice of William Greenway who recommends that we should acknowledge "the profound offense" of suffering and concede the Enlightenment argument.[1] "Christians," writes Greenway, "are not distinguished by having a theory which

---

1. Greenway, "Cosomodicy," 4.

adequately accounts for evil. *No one* has such a theory."[2] Christians live by faith. That does not make faith blind to suffering or unreasonable in the face of it. To the contrary, faith opens our eyes, revealing suffering more starkly in every dimension including not only its givenness but also our complicity, a "conundrum"(Greenway's term) radically voiced by both Testaments as evidenced by Jeremiah, Job, the psalmist, among a host of others, not the least of whom is the Crucified.

Faith seeks understanding, not plausibility established by reason which reduces God to a logically deduced ideal that may be known apart from faith, a project that turns God into an idol making grace null and void. God is not an object in the universe subject to observation among other objects. Accordingly, followers of Christ meet suffering by testimony to hope grounded in the crucified and living Lord.

Given the confines of this chapter, I have collapsed suffering, sin, evil, nothingness, and death under the rubric "not good," a symbol of what opposes, resists, and contradicts God's desire. Under this rubric I will consider four aspects of creation: contingency, companionship, choice, and agency. To begin I want to return to Genesis by continuing reflections begun in chapter 6.

Like many I was taught that God created a paradise from which we fell and to which we will one day return. Meanwhile, we live with faith as best we can between paradise lost and regained. This working meta-narrative sustained me through college and graduate school and with modifications shaped forty years of Christian ministry. While the model is not altogether wrong, upon a closer reading of Genesis and in view of twenty-first-century science, guided by a Reformed theological perspective, I have come to understand this core conviction differently. In brief, humans did not fall from paradise. Rather, we are born into a "very good" creation imperiled by "not good." Creation is "very good" but not perfect. Things are not the way they are supposed to be or how they could be.

In my youth I was taught, as perhaps you may have been, that something must account for the imperfections repeatedly appearing in creation. I was taught and so I imagined that humans messed up paradise. We rebelled and our fall, our sin, allowed "not good" to enter creation.

I am not arguing that we are not fallen or sinful or that creation is not systemically and structurally marred and distorted by sin. I concur with Paul when he says that "all have sinned and fall short of the glory of God" (Rom 3:23). However, I do not read Paul's argument that "sin came into the world through one man" (Rom 5:12) as evidence of a literal historical fall

---

2. Greenway, "Cosomodicy," 6.

which accounts for the presence of suffering. All humans sin; and death is a consequence of sin. Yet, I am persuaded that suffering cannot be attributed to human rebellion alone. Suffering is a given of creation. Creation is "very good" but not perfect or complete or as it shall be.

FAITH SEEKING UNDERSTANDING

How can I give you up, Ephraim? How can I hand you over O Israel? . . . I am God and no mortal. —Hos 11:8–9

The God who creates cannot and does not walk away from God's "very good" but imperfect creation which is burdened with and opposed by "not good." (This citation and those that follow in this section may be found in Genesis 2:4b—3:24.) Mortals may and do abandon their works, but not God. God refuses to let "not good" define creation. The work of not leaving creation imperfect begins when God stakes a *No Trespassing* sign in the middle of the garden. The sign defines a danger in creation while establishing a protective limit for the benefit of God's creatures. Paradise is not exactly paradise. It has trees which are "pleasant to the sight and good for food"; there is even a "tree of life" from which we may "freely eat." But there is also a dangerous tree in the garden, "the tree of the knowledge of good and evil."

    The garden is incomplete. Genesis doesn't explain why this is so. The dangerous, deadly tree is a given along with "every tree that is pleasant to the sight and good for food." God grants full and complete access to the good and pleasant trees, including the "tree of life" that is "in the midst of the garden." Abundance, which generates flourishing, resides with a single restriction, "but of the tree of the knowledge of good and evil you shall not eat, for in the day that you eat of it you shall die." The garden sponsors human flourishing, but it is not a perfect paradise. Creation is laden with contingency, both moral and creaturely. We do not know why this is so; it is simply a given of creaturely existence.

    The second marker that the garden is "very good" but not perfect is disclosed by God's verdict that it is "*not good* that the man should be alone." God addresses this imperfection by creating "a helper." The helper is not ancillary or secondary much less subsidiary to the man of dust. Scripture regularly and frequently defines God as our *help*. The text is not proscribing roles for males and females. The text draws attention to loneliness, which is different from solitude and more akin to isolation or incompleteness. Aloneness represents the second aspect of "not good" in creation which is to say that we are human only in relation to other humans. Humans require companions. Companionship is essential to being human. Loneliness contradicts God's purpose.

The third and fourth aspects of the "not good" of creation are brought to light by the exchange between the man and his wife and the talking snake; namely, choices are limited and agency is finite. While tradition supplies multiple theories about the snake's presence, purpose, and origin, Genesis intriguingly states that the "serpent was more crafty than any other wild animal that *the LORD God had made*." The talking snake is created by God. The snake offhandedly invites the helper to consider God's desire: "Did God say, 'You shall not eat from any tree in the garden?'"

The talking snake draws attention to God's prohibition rather than God's permission. We suspect the talking snake is prodding a presumed pliable victim. We may not be wrong in the assumption, for the helper responds, though not as predictably as expected. The helper answers the snake's not so innocuous inquiry by recounting a version of God's command, which brings into view a fourth aspect of creation—the helper and the living being are created with agency, a capacity to trust and mistrust. Humans do not acquire agency after *the fall*. Agency precedes *the fall*.

The helper tells the talking snake that the garden has many trees from which she and her husband may freely eat. While the helper acknowledges God's permission her reply reveals a darker sentiment, "We may eat of the fruit of the trees in the garden," she says, "but God said, 'You shall not eat of the fruit of the tree that is in the middle of the garden, nor shall you *touch* it, or you will die.'" The helper resents the safeguard. God's prohibitive command did not forbid touching. Creation is "very good," but the Creator limits choice. The helper resents the restriction and so will her husband.

In round two, the talking snake moves from raising suspicion to making accusations while offering reassurance couched in god-speak. "You will not die," the snake coolly observes. To the contrary, "God knows that when you eat of it your eyes will be opened, and you will be like God . . ." The accusation from the resident theologian brings the helper's dynamic and cogent agency into full view. The helper's decision is well considered, "The tree was good for food . . . a delight to the eyes . . . and desired to make one wise." Having considered the merits, the helper "took of its fruit and ate" and without hesitation or persuasion she also gave some to her husband, and he ate. The carefully deliberated choice, which appeared good, turned out to be not so good—eyes were opened but the helper and her husband were not made God-like. Ashamed, the pair made coverings for their naked vulnerabilities and hid from the presence of God.

There are consequences to decisions made by the helper and her husband traditionally headed under the caption of *the fall*. While that designation may be useful as a signature for the power of sin and its consequences, it distracts from the givens of creation which *precede* the consequences precipitated by the mistrust of helper and her husband. These givens of creation offer a more accurate depiction of the human predicament than those captured by terms like paradise or pre-fall creation, which, in light of experience and science sound fanciful and false. Genesis is not science but it does further understanding. And the understanding it sponsors depicts a world we are familiar with, one which "remains open to a number of possibilities" in which our "creaturely activity will prove crucial for the development of the world."[3]

Creation is freighted with contingency, some of which is morally deadly. Other forms of contingency are equally deadly but cohere with creatureliness, contingencies like earthquakes or heart tissues which harden and cells which mutate into cancers. Companionship, though essential to our humanness, when coupled with poor judgment, may result in disaster. Creation is good enough for flourishing but ironically and tragically, companionship and contingency, which make dynamic, adaptive, and moral life possible, also bring distrust and death.

Creation is good enough for flourishing but is not perfect enough to arrest suffering. You and I have choices. We also enjoy agency. Choice plus agency does not always result in good. Creation is "very good" but not perfect and is made less so by our distrust of God's desire.

Creation is not solely a stage for the helper and the man of dust. Another figure appears—indeed, this Other creates the stage. The Creator of the stage does not stand apart from the helper and her husband. This Other is not dispassionate or aloof but walks alongside the hiding humans seeking and questioning them. The helper and her husband not only command this Other's attention, company, and conversation but also alarm, protection, and deliverance. The Creator will not abide by human separation, shame, and hiding. The Creator enters the garden as Redeemer.

DELIVERANCE; ASYMMETRY REVISITED

I have observed the misery of my people who are in Egypt; I have heard their cry on account of their taskmasters. Indeed, I know their sufferings, and I have come down to deliver them . . . —Exod 3:7–8

---

3. Fretheim, "Genesis," in Brueggeman et al., *General and Old Testament Articles*, 346.

Redemption does not begin with Moses, or Abraham before him, or even Noah prior to Abraham. Redemption begins when God separates the light from the darkness. Redemption continues when God addresses the "not good" of loneliness, which exemplifies a trinitarian conviction expressed in chapter 1: all of God is involved in all of God's works. For purposes of thinking about faith, creation and redemption are separated. In reality they are different sides of one coin. God redeems creation. Alternately, creation is God's work of redemption.

Deliverance or redemption is God's work of new creation. The God who redeems as Paul writes "calls into existence the things that do not exist" (Rom 4:17). Consider the deliverance of Abraham's children from Egyptian oppression. God "comes down to deliver," but redeems his people by calling Moses, a murderer on the run to lead the oppressed to freedom. Deliverance will be accompanied by signs and wonders but also faithful response expressed by a people of hope who trudge through muddy waters and a dry, barren wilderness, people who stumble and fall and get back up to march toward freedom.

Consider Jesus who teaches disciples to pray daily, saying, "Do not bring us to the time of trial, but rescue us from the evil one" (Matt 6:13). Consider also that Jesus taught his disciples that they should not worry about food and drink and clothing or shelter because God knows they need these things (Matt 6:25–33). God is not unaware of contingency or loneliness or limited choice or yet again of our finite agency. When the disciples complain to Jesus that the people accompanying them are hungry, Jesus directs the disciples, saying, "You give them something to eat" (Mark 6:37). Consider finally the crucified God who does not get a last-minute reprieve though a legion of angels is available to rescue him (Matt 26:53). Jesus teaches that all things are possible with God, yet evil and suffering are not magically removed from creation. God does not annihilate creation. God redeems and provides for creation, a topic for chapter 14 when the meaning of prayer will be explored.

LAMENT, PROTEST, AND HEALING

Comfort, O comfort my people, says your God. . . . Get you up to a high mountain, O Zion, herald of good tidings; lift up your voice with strength, O Jerusalem, herald of good tidings, lift it up, do not fear; say to the cities of Judah, "Here is your God!" —Isa 40:1, 9

Jeremiah recognized the emptiness of crying peace when wounds are treated carelessly (Jer 6:14). Heralds of good tidings protest suffering and bring healing but they also lament the "not good" of creation. Heralds lament as co-sufferers. Lament does not gloss over suffering but precedes good tidings which are voiced "with strength." Heralds do not countenance or flee from suffering. "Comfort," to use Isaiah's word, comes when followers "get up" and publicly proclaim good news. Protest, or public testimony, does not come separate and apart from suffering with those who suffer. Protest is embodied by those who love the Crucified. Followers of the Crucified do not love the cross—they love Jesus and because they love Jesus they despise the cross.[4] Christian faith does not valorize suffering. Christian faith seeks to heal suffering.

The World Health Organization estimated 2016 worldwide deaths at nearly sixty million. Seven in ten deaths were attributed to non-communicable disease. Heart disease and cancer account for nearly one-half of non-communicable disease. Our bodies break down. We are subject to creaturely contingency.

Suffering is also attributable to moral contingency. In 2016, twelve million people died prematurely because they lacked adequate medicine, sanitation, and/or nutrition. Additionally, slightly more people died from accidents than from addiction, suicide, and violence combined. Lastly, in the same year, just over seven thousand died from natural disasters, a historically low number in view of the ten-year annual average of over twenty-two thousand as reported by the International Federation of Red Cross and Red Crescent Societies.[5] I will return to human caused suffering in the next chapter on justice; here I want to make several observations about suffering and moral accountability.

The earth moves; storms rage; cells divide; viruses live; accidents happen; moral decisions are made. While contingency limits our options or choices, suffering can be mitigated by moral decisions such as more equitable distribution of nutrition, sanitation, and medicine. While our agency is finite, suffering can be reduced when fewer of us live near seacoasts or on fault lines or in flood-prone river valleys or near areas subject to annual wildfires. And, when we do live in high risk locations, increased measures can be taken to reduce harm from *natural* disasters or *acts of God* which are more accurately named *human*-made disasters resulting from flawed planning and stewardship. Rivers cannot be blamed for flooding any more than

---

4. Moltmann, *The Crucified God*, 1.
5. Ritchie and Roser, "Causes of Death."

God can be blamed when houses built on ocean shorelines are destroyed by hurricanes.

In the epoch of the Anthropocene, given what we know about human impacts on our planet, humans can prevent, reduce, and ameliorate suffering directly caused by our misuse and overuse of the biosphere. Alternative energy strategies and reduced resource consumption, among other wise responses which respect the limits of the "very good" creation the Creator creates, will reduce suffering.

Even with these and other steps, suffering is a given of human existence. Even good death in a ripe old age brings sorrow. Just as God does not walk away from the "not good" of creation, so people of faith do not walk away. We lament with those who lament. We suffer with those who suffer. And when and where we can, we do something about it—hope sponsors healing. And where physical healing is not possible, we witness to "the peace of God, which surpasses all understanding . . ." (Phil 4:7). The Creator calls us to join him in making all things new by participating in the work of redemption through lament, protest, and works of healing.

Ultimate, final healing will be addressed in chapter 20. In the next chapter, I will continue the present discussion as we consider the contours and power of justice which foster provisional healing in this pen-ultimate time called *today*.

Chapter 12

Is There No Justice?

HOW LONG?

O LORD, how long shall I cry for help, and you will not listen? Or cry to you 'Violence!' and you will not save? Why do you make me see wrongdoing and look at trouble? Destruction and violence are before me; strife and contention arise. So the law becomes slack and justice never prevails. The wicked surround the righteous—therefore judgment comes forth perverted. —Hab 1:2–4

Imagine Youssef and Mariam—their eight-year-old son died when he let go of their hands and darted from a sidewalk onto a busy street and was crushed by a passing car. Two years later Mariam and Youssef's fourteen-year-old daughter died when a rocket attack destroyed the market where she had gone to buy bread. When their son died, Youssef and Mariam asked, *Why?* When their daughter died, they asked, *How long?* Both prayers were anguished and addressed the same God. With time, the first sorrow grew bittersweet. The second remained simply bitter. What does justice look like for Youssef and Mariam? What does justice look like for those who launched the attack?

Or consider a thirteen-year-old teen I will name Akachi (ah-KAH-chi). Her name means *God's Hand*. Akachi is an orphan living in Wajir, a county seat of one hundred thousand in a northeastern province of Kenya bordering Somalia. As a consequence of her prolonged iron-deficient diet, Akachi's IQ is sixty-nine. Eighty-four percent of her county's seven hundred thousand residents live in absolute poverty. What does justice look like for Akachi and for the people of her province? What does justice look like for near and distant neighbors who hear about Akachi's plight and that of her people? How will they, how should we, respond in justice?

In the previous chapter, I considered four aspects of creation: contingency, companionship, choice, and agency. These conditions which influence understandings of suffering also apply to justice. What does justice look like for a thirteen-year-old like Akachi living in a drought-stricken land torn by civil unrest and intermittent warfare? What does justice look like for this girl whose companionship is compromised by the loss of her family; a young person whose choices are limited by poverty, education, job training, and employment; a teenager whose agency is compromised not only by inadequate social structures but also diminished intelligence? Akachi's plight is extreme but tragically not exceptional. Worldwide, one billion human beings are trapped in absolute poverty resembling fourteenth-century living conditions. What does justice look like for these inhabitants of Earth and millions like Akachi? What does it look like for tens of thousands like Miriam and Youssef? What does justice look like for any, including readers of this book, who cry, *How long?*

We are justified by God to do justice. Doing justice is not an afterthought to justification. Justice making or doing justice, like being healed and healing, coheres with being justified or made righteous. "The one who is righteous," Paul says quoting Habakkuk, "will live by faith" (Rom 1:17). What does it mean to live by faith righteously or to do justice within the conditions of creation?

In what follows I will define creative justice which unites God's creating and redeeming work. I gratefully acknowledge the writings of Jürgen Moltmann which inform my efforts. Unlike distributive and retributive justice, founded upon law, creative justice is brought by God's grace. The former judges what is; the latter creates what will be. The former rewards merits and punishes deserts; the latter establishes righteousness. The former employs coercion; the latter overcomes evil with good. Creative justice does not leverage reward and punishment but leavens all things with grace, making them new. Creative justice intends redemption for victims and perpetrators while redressing structures and powers which generate victims and perpetrators alike.

In this chapter I will explore the foundations of creative justice through a reading of the story of Cain and Abel before considering the character of creative justice in a section titled "Not Long—Waiting and Hastening."

In the concluding section, I will outline the contours of justice and mercy birthed by Pentecost hope.

Creative justice touches upon every aspect of living. Chapter 13 on the neighbor will consider civil and social justice; chapter 17 on work will be occupied by reflections on economic and ecological justice; chapter 18 on God and country will address national and global justice and state sanctioned retribution. To begin, I invite you to consider how God's creative justice emerges amid the sibling rivalry of the children of Adam and Eve.

THAT'S NOT FAIR!

In the course of time Cain brought to the LORD an offering of the fruit of the ground, and Abel for his part brought of the firstlings of his flock, their fat portions. And the LORD had regard for Abel and his offering, but for Cain and his offering he had no regard. So Cain was very angry, and his countenance fell. —Gen 4:3–5

The Bible presents an unblinkered depiction of the connections between sin, evil, suffering, nothingness, and death. If injustice can emerge within kinship, imagine the complications when it emerges beyond kinship. From the Bible's telling, injustice rears its ugly head before humans encounter the truly other—the neighbor, the outsider, the stranger, the sojourning alien, the enemy. Injustice emerges within the family that prays together. While the story of Cain and Abel (Gen 4:1–16) is marred by tragedy, it is not eclipsed by it. Though bloodied by the blood he spills, Cain continues to live, even if east of Eden in *Wanderland*.

Cain is the firstborn. His name means "to get, to create," as expressed by Eve's shout of praise upon his birth, "I have produced a man with the help of the LORD." Abel, a name meaning "vapor, nothingness," is born without fanfare. As his name suggests, there is nothing special about Abel whose birth is distinguished only by a passing reference to his elder brother— "Next she bore his brother Abel."

The siblings differ not only by birth but also vocation. Curiously, the younger is mentioned first, "Abel was a keeper of sheep, and Cain a tiller of the ground." The priority may betray a cultural bias toward shepherding or may reflect an incidental narrative move. We hear nothing definitive about the siblings, nothing about the quality of their work, nothing of their moral character or interests or abilities. The narrative moves immediately to worship where in "the course of time Cain brought an offering of the fruit of the ground, and Abel for his part brought the firstlings of his flock, their fat portions."

Many interpreters propose backstories which account for God's coming judgment. The text itself is silent. God's judgment is rendered without account, "And the LORD had regard for Abel and his offering, but for Cain and his offering he had no regard." The narrative leaves Cain, along with the reader, hanging—why this strange verdict? Why was Cain's offering displeasing or was it displeasingly offered? We are not told. We do not see behind the curtain. God's judgment remains inscrutable. That very inscrutability is interpreted by Cain as divine injustice.

Cain's reading of God's verdict is betrayed by undisguised anger and disappointment. Cain believed he deserved to be rewarded for his offering. God has violated Cain's moral calculus. Cain believed his offering merited regard. His distressed face cries out, *Not fair!* Before Cain can express moral outrage over the perceived injustice, God questions the one born with God's help and offers resolution, "Why are you angry [Cain], and why has your countenance fallen? If you do well, will you not be accepted? And if you do not do well, sin is lurking at the door; its desire is for you but you must master it."

Cain has a problem. Cain's problem is not Abel. His problem is God. Aware of the problem, God intervenes. Will the intervention succeed? Will God's invitation and encouragement arrest Cain's anger and ameliorate his despair? Will Cain's God problem resolve before morphing into a lethal brother problem?

Like his parents, Cain enjoys agency and options. He is not predisposed to a predetermined outcome. Despite protests by lapsarian original sin advocates, Cain may accept God's invitation and master that which preys upon him. Finite though it may be, Cain has agency. God trusts Cain to render a right decision. Sin, which lies in wait for Cain, not unlike the talking snake which tricked his parents, is a predator possessing corrupting desire. God insists that Cain "must master it." Tragically, despite his desire, encouragement, and entreaty, God's intervention fails. Cain refuses God's bidding to "do well." Cain does not master the predator but instead invites his willing and unsuspecting brother to "go out to the field" and there Cain "rose up against his brother Abel and killed him."

The God who renders a judgement at worship, the God who warns of sin's deadly danger, the God who desires good, does not restrain the possibility of evil. It is a mystery. Why doesn't God restrain Cain instead of entreating and encouraging and trusting him to master sin? Why does God give Cain such unbridled freedom? Alternately, why does God give the predator (sin) such unrestrained access to Cain? What rational, law-abiding judge would permit such unrestraint? The narrative remains silent.

In due time, order will come through law to Cain's descendants. Redeemed slaves will enter a wilderness where divine laws will be given. The freed will eventually settle the promised land, establish a kingdom, and, from time to time, reform it by calling for returns to holy lawfulness, but finally the law-guided state will collapse. Does God fail to anticipate the consequences of his judgments and decrees? Are God's laws inadequate to restrain sin? Do humans, cooperating with sin, overrule God's purpose, pushing aside God's warnings and laws and perhaps even aspects of God's sovereignty such as restraint? However we answer, God does not simply capitulate and watch the train wreck, not even after the murder is committed.

As in the garden, following tragic mistrust, God draws near the sinner posing a question, "Where is your brother Abel?" Like his parents before him, Cain answers with a lie, "I don't know." Again, like his parents, he then blames the Creator: "Am I my brother's keeper?" Cain knows, as we know, as the psalmist knew, that God is our "keeper. . . . The LORD will keep you from all evil; he will keep your life" (Ps 121:5–7). Cain charges God with falling down on his job. Abel's death is not Cain's fault. Fault is assigned to the Keeper of Life.

The diversion fails. The Creator first accuses Cain, "What have you done?" And then asserts, before Cain can answer, that the elder should hear what God has heard, "Listen; your brother's blood is crying out to me from the ground!" While God does not restrain the perpetrator, neither does he ignore the consequence of his action. God hears. Without pause to ascertain if Cain is listening, God also judges: "And now you are cursed from the ground, which has opened its mouth to receive your brother's blood from your hand. When you till the ground, it will no longer yield to you its strength; you will be a fugitive and a wanderer on the earth."

I will return to the "curse from the ground" in chapter 17. Here I wish to lift up the creative justice of God. Cain names God's initial verdict *punishment*. Cain laments that his punishment "is greater" than he can bear, the sentence too heavy. "Today you have driven me away from the soil," Cain pleads, "and I shall be hidden from your face; I shall be a fugitive and a wanderer on the earth, and anyone who meets me may kill me."

In a surprise reversal, God amends his initial intention. Has Cain demonstrated remorse or is he merely fearful that his vulnerability will be exposed, or perhaps both? Whatever the case, God responds to his plea: "Not so! Whoever kills Cain will suffer a sevenfold vengeance." God then "put a mark on Cain, so that no one who came upon him would kill him." God protects the wandering murderer. Just deserts are overridden by unmerited grace. As Christian baptism will one day signify, Cain is marked by guilt and grace.

After receiving the twofold signature of grace and guilt, the narrative does not say that God withdraws from Cain, but tragically that "Cain went away from the presence of the LORD, and settled in the land of Nod, east of Eden." The Hebrew word *Nod* means "wander." Cain settles in *Wanderland*. That Cain "settles" in *Wanderland* inclines interpretation toward restlessness rather than nomadic or semi-nomadic life. As Augustine understood, "Our hearts are restless until they rest in Thee." Readers sense a story is not ending but beginning.

Creative justice, even for a murderer like Cain, establishes the possibility of newness. Though cursed from the ground and exiled into restlessness, there is grace for the fugitive murderer. A burden is made lighter for Cain. This biblical narrative only addresses the perpetrator. We must wait for other narratives which open possibilities for victims. Even so, this narrative establishes a fundamental feature of creative justice—God's grace creates unseen and unforeseen possibilities out of impossibilities too burdensome to bear.

NOT LONG—WAITING AND HASTENING

The Lord is not slow about his promise, as some think of slowness, but is patient with you, not wanting any to perish but all to come to repentance. —2 Pet 3:9

Second Peter, dating well into the second century, is likely the last book written in the New Testament. Regardless of the precise originating date, the writer lived in a time when the first and likely the second and even portions of a third generation of Christians have died since the death and resurrection and promised return of Jesus. Readers or listeners have grown impatient and weary. God's time and their time are out of sync, which prompts the people of God to lament, "Where is the promise of his coming? For ever since our ancestors died, all things continue as they were from the beginning of creation!" (2 Pet 3:4). Peter's congregation, disappointed by the delayed return of Jesus, sounds like the late fourth to mid-third-century-BCE Teacher or Assembly Leader of Ecclesiastes who sighs, "What has been is what will be, and what has been done is what will be done; there is nothing new under the sun" (Eccl 1:9).

Like Cain, Peter's congregation is disappointed if not angry—God has not delivered as they understood promised deliverance. Nothing had changed. The world continued as if Jesus had not appeared. The world appeared indifferent and unimpressed by God's mighty work of resurrection. Following Jesus seemed to be much ado about nothing. Peter attempts to redress this lament by adjusting perceptions of time: "Do not ignore this one fact, beloved, that with the Lord one day is like a thousand years, and a thousand years are like one day." God, reasons Peter, does not count time as we count time: "The Lord is not slow about his promise, as some think of slowness . . ." (2 Pet 3:8–9).

How do we compare our time with God's time? In chapter 5 a compressed time scale of 13.8 years was used to help us imagine the 13.8 billion-year-old cosmos we inhabit. Peter may be using a similar device when he says that "with the Lord one day is like a thousand years." The device intends to help listeners see their circumstance from God's perspective. You may be experiencing injustice, Peter seems to be saying, but rest assured, all is well and is part of God's long-term promise to bring all to repentance so that no one perishes.

While the aim is noble and accentuates the gracious purpose of God, the device may offer but cold comfort to Peter's struggling congregants much less to oppressed teens like Akachi or bereaved parents like Youssef and Miriam or to most any of us when injustice weighs heavily. How do we reconcile God's time with our time? Alternately, how is God's love married to God's justice? Peter answers that we live by hope "waiting and hastening the coming day of God" (2 Pet 3:12). Peter's testimony raises the question: What does "waiting and hastening" mean? What does that look like?

Hastening looks like a shepherd who leaves the ninety-nine in the wilderness and with urgency searches for the one that was lost. Upon finding the lost, he lays it on his shoulders and rejoices. Upon returning he calls together his friends, inviting them to rejoice with him. Hastening looks like a woman who carefully sweeps her house clean and does not rest until she finds a lost coin. Upon finding it, she too calls together her friends, and rejoices. Hastening looks like the prodigal's father who runs to welcome his lost younger son. Upon the younger's return, the father kills the fatted calf and invites friends to celebrate (Luke 15:1–32). Hastening is urgent but not frantic, persistent but not dire. Hastening brims with determined joy.

The reign of God is hastened when we do God's will on earth as it is done in heaven. Hastening anticipates the kingdom by living now what shall be when the King arrives. Waiting is the patient work of persevering in hastening. Like love, waiting "bears all things, believes all things, hopes, all things, endures all things" (1 Cor 13:7). Waiting is not measured by success but by faithfully loving and doing justice despite present circumstances.

Peter was right when he said that one day, from our perspective, looks like a thousand years from God's perspective. We experience time one day at a time. We live moment to moment, remembering the past while imagining the future. Past, present, and future do not apply to God. Our sojourn passes swiftly in a succession of moments like a "weaver's shuttle" (Job 7:6). With Abel we are vapor. Like vanishing morning mist, we live between memory and imagination, subject to what the Greeks called *chronos* or clock time. But we also experience what the Greeks named *kairos* or the right or critical or opportune time or what Jesus named "fulfilled" time.

We live by chronos when we set our alarm for 6:00 a.m. We live by kairos when we have a good time or when time stands still or when we think a moment will never end or when we wish one would never end. Kairos invades chronos when we glimpse moments of what shall be for all moments. Kairos collapses past-present-future. We saw this when Jesus took up the Isaiah scroll and after reading announced, "Today this scripture has been fulfilled in your hearing" (Luke 4:21). The promised reign of God draws us toward the future made present in Jesus. Whenever we repair or remake or heal a damaged past we anticipate God's reign. Promoted by future reconciliation, forgiveness heals the past. We are capable of living in kairos; we simply do not and cannot remain there. We are mortal and not God. We live between chronos and kairos, a tension Peter expressed when he observes that our time and God's time are not the same.

God's love creates justice and God's justice creates love which we express by "hastening." We hasten the reign of God when we love justly and justly love in accord with the image of the invisible God made visible in Jesus Christ. Jesus is the first and last expression of loving justice or just love. In this hour, and this is the conundrum expressed by Peter's lamenting congregation, which is not unlike the complaint voiced by Habakkuk seven hundred years earlier, we cry, "How long?" How long must we hasten?

Kairos inevitably collides with chronos, which means that creative justice is provisional. Because creative justice is provisional, we don't simply hasten, we wait. Hastening and waiting are joined. Hastening is qualified by waiting. And waiting is qualified by hastening. Creative justice expresses both qualities.

Our hastening is quickened by the promise of God's coming and is tempered by waiting which means it is durable. Hastening tempered by waiting does not "faint or grow weary" because God "does not faint or grow weary" (Isa 40:28). Faith hastens the day of the Lord while we wait for "new heavens and a new earth, where righteousness is at home" (2 Pet 3:13).

WHEN JUSTICE AND MERCY MEET

Now to one who works, wages are not reckoned as a gift but as something due. But to one who without works trusts him who justifies the ungodly, such faith is reckoned as righteousness. —Romans 4:4–5

Anchored in law, distributive and retributive justice alternately rewards or punishes. Law-based justice throws us solely onto ourselves. If, as Cain believed, we are judged by law, faith in a merciful and just God is not required. The good news of the Bible is that God judges by mercy. God is both just and merciful.

We are not saved by following law. We are saved by God's creative justice or mercy. In the next chapter, I will explore how mercy takes shape in loving neighbors justly. Here I want to anticipate what will be said more fully in the next chapter; namely, creative justice is the work of the Holy Spirit. This claim was announced on the day of Pentecost when Peter, citing the prophet Joel, testified, "In the last days it will be, God declares, that I will pour out my Spirit upon all flesh. . . . Then everyone who calls on the name of the Lord shall be saved" (Acts 2:17, 21).

Just as there is no Pentecost without Easter so there is no Easter without Pentecost. Creative justice, which hastens and waits for the reign of God, is the work of the Father, by the Son, through the Spirit. Creative justice is driven by the Spirit who gives life to the dead and calls into existence things which do not exist. The Spirit does not leave sinners in the condition in which they were found. Mercy changes us. The Spirit newly makes victims and perpetrators. The Spirit summons each to get up, to stand, and walk toward God's desired reconciliation and peace. God's creative justice creates choice where none before existed. God's creative justice liberates us from the confines of finite agency giving will-power once deemed impossible. God's creative justice does not settle for gentle acceptance of moral and creaturely contingency as status quo. God's Spirit has been poured out on all flesh to renew all human beings, indeed creation. In the following chapter, this Pentecost hope will be explored through civil and social justice among neighbors.

POSTSCRIPT

Five years after the rocket attack, Youssef and Mariam adopted four-year-old twins whose parents were killed in a separate attack. While bitterness lingers in their household, laughter is slowly returning. With Mariam's encouragement, Youssef reluctantly signed on for a locally sponsored program called *Bridges* designed to reconcile rivals. Ariel, a thirty-six-year-old retired battery commander, weary of nightmares and hangovers, enrolled about the same time. Though they do not know one another, each wonders what the day will hold should they meet. Both are hastening and waiting for the Spirit.

Akachi, now eighteen, works in a nearby climate-smart cooperative. The greenhouse, which uses drip irrigation, grows vegetables, which Akachi tends and harvests. Akachi still lives at the orphanage. She, along with three house mothers, helps twenty school-age girls who share the house. Akachi calls it home.

Creative justice through the Spirit is bringing newness for Akachi and Youssef and Miriam and Ariel . . . newness which dares to hope and live in the face of injustice and suffering.

Chapter 13

Who Is My Neighbor?

NEIGHBOR

A man was going down from Jerusalem to Jericho, and fell into the hands of robbers, who stripped him, beat him, and went away, leaving him half dead. —Luke 10:30

Vantage. Noun. Definition—a place or position affording a good view of something.

Jesus invites us to imagine a robbery on an isolated road. We are the victim. We have been beaten and bloodied and left for dead. Imagine the humiliation and vulnerability, the taste of rust in your mouth, the arresting dread that your attackers may return, the bone-wearying loneliness of coming night. Assume that desperate vantage.

Maybe approaching darkness will bring relief or perhaps only cover for wild dogs howling in the distance? Will you survive the night? And if you don't, who will know, who will care, who will tell your family? Will someone provide for your children? These are your dying thoughts. And then you hear distant but distinct hoof beats growing stronger. They suddenly stop. A figure standing by a donkey silhouetted by fading sunlight, calls out: *Hey, you all right over there?* Through matted eyes you manage a nod as the stranger covers your wounded body while lifting water to your cracked lips.

Neighbor. Noun. Definition—a person who shows mercy.

"What must I *do*?" Jesus stands firmly in the tradition of the prophet Micah who, in response to that question, answered that we are required "to *do* justice, and to love kindness, and to walk humbly with [our] God" (Micah 6:8). Jesus invites us to see neighbor love from the vantage of the victim. He directs us to understand God's justice and love as recipients of kindness.

Not once but three times Moses reminded the children of Abraham to remember they were once slaves in Egypt. Moses connected that deep traumatic memory not only with generosity toward fellow Israelites but also with the treatment of widows, orphans, strangers, and resident aliens (Deut 15:15; 16:12; 24:17). Remember you were slaves, Moses exhorts Israel. Remember your suffering and the kindness of God which delivered you. Jesus, likewise, invited his listeners to see the world through the eyes of those who suffer. Assume that vantage, he says, and you will know something of the inexhaustible fellowship of the Father, Son, and Holy Spirit. "Only the suffering God can help."[1] We do justice; we love kindness and walk humbly with God from the vantage of suffering.

CREATIVE JUSTICE

"Which of these three, do you think, was a neighbor to the man who fell into the hands of the robbers?" He said, "The one who showed him mercy." Jesus said to him, "Go and do likewise." —Luke 10:36–37

Unlike law-based justice which distributes and repays from a limited fund, creative justice multiplies possibility by drawing from the unlimited treasury of God's mercy. Law-based justice divides and repays. God's creative justice transforms.

Retributive justice and distributive justice share the Latin root *tribuere* (pay or tribute). Both assume that tribute is scarce. *Dis*tributive justice divides limited tribute; *re*tributive justice pays it back. Pay and payback are routinely measured in one of five ways. (1) Equality—everybody gets the same tribute regardless of input. (2) Equity—tribute should equal input. (3) Power—those with more authority, status, control, or responsibility receive greater tribute. (4) Need—those with the greatest need receive tribute regardless of their input. (5) Responsibility—those with more tribute should share with those who have less.[2]

Retributive justice follows a similar moral logic. It repays tribute that has been taken. The law of retaliation or "an eye for an eye" expressed in the

---

1. Bonhoeffer, *Letters & Papers from Prison*, 360.
2. Wikipedia, "Justice as Fairness."

Babylonian Code of Hammurabi (1754 BCE) and reflected in Exod 21:23 limited payback. Tribute paid back should not exceed initiating injury or insult in order to compensate loss. The law of *lex talionis* asserted that punishments should fit crimes. In his Sermon on the Mount, Jesus referred to a version of this ancient code. After citing it, he taught, "But I say to you, Do not resist an evildoer. But if anyone strikes you on the right cheek, turn the other also . . ." (Matt 5:39). Do not repay evil with evil, Jesus says, overcome evil with mercy.

Jesus shifts the basis of moral logic from law to mercy—not tit for tat, not measure for measure, but abundant kindness in all relationships, even impossibly difficult ones. Jesus makes this shift not once but six times in the Sermon on the Mount, the signature expression of his moral reasoning. That ethic culminates in his radical extension of kindness to the enemy: "You have heard that it was said, 'You shall love your neighbor and hate your enemy.' But I say to you, 'Love your enemies and pray for those who persecute you . . ." (Matt 5:43–44).

The theology of Jesus' ethic is plainly stated, "Your Father in heaven . . . makes his sun rise on the evil and on the good, and sends rain on the righteous and the unrighteous" (Matt 5:45). God does not pick and choose recipients of his benevolence. Deserving and loss are not factors in the equation of God's love. Tribute is not divided or repaid by God nor should it be among those who follow Jesus. Kindness, Jesus teaches, is not scarce but abundant. Creative justice is never exhausted. It opens victims and perpetrators alike to a previously unimagined future, one defined by God's mercy.

Mercy moves us from loathing and enmity to loving and peace. Mercy transforms misery and irritability to joy and patience. Mercy moves the cruel and greedy to kindness and generosity. Mercy reduces brutality to gentleness and infidelity to faithfulness. It turns self-indulgence and arrogance to self-control and humility. The acquiescent and fearful are made defiant and courageous. The indifferent are brought to compassion. Mercy creates beauty where ugliness once reigned. Neighbor love lifts up others and while doing so refuses to create dependency.

Jerusalem is on a hill. Jericho is in a hole—the Jordan Rift Valley terminates at the Dead Sea, the lowest land elevation on Earth. Travelers from Jerusalem to Jericho descend. Neighbors descend. The Samaritan not only descended from Jerusalem—he stoops to help the bloodied and beaten victim. The posture is significant. It is not unlike the descent of Jesus beautifully described in the early hymn Paul cited in his Letter to the Philippians where Paul invited Christians to have the "same mind" that was in Christ Jesus. Christ, Paul explains, "did not regard equality with God as something to be exploited, but emptied himself taking the form of a slave. And being in human form, he humbled himself to the point of death—even death on a cross" (Phil 2:5–8).

Neighbors help from below—not from above, but on bended knees. The posture of neighbor love stands receivers on their feet restoring their dignity, worth, and agency. When the Samaritan gets the victim to safety he advances payment for his care and promises to return to settle any additional debt. He does not stick around to receive accolades but moves on. The helper recedes from view. Neighbor love is self-effacing. When justice is done, help is given and received and heaven rejoices.

THE ROYAL LAW

You do well if you really fulfill the royal law according to the scripture. "You shall love your neighbor as yourself." —Jas 2:8

"You *do well* if you really fulfill the royal law." We met this expression when we overheard God encouraging Cain, "And if you *do well*, will you not be accepted?" (Gen 4:7). Here, generations later, we hear it again—we *do well* when we love neighbors. For those made in the image of God it is a fitting rule—the *royal* law—the law that governs those who represent God.

We are God's representatives. We do well when we love neighbors made in the image of God. There are no restrictions, no limits, no non-neighbors. The royal law dissolves distinctions made by nature and nurture which are routinely used to restrict kindness. The Apostle Paul put it this way, "There is no longer Jew or Greek, there is no longer slave or free, there is no longer male and female, for all of you are one in Christ Jesus" (Gal 3:28). Neighbor love is unrestricted.

Paul, the former persecutor of Christians, cannot be accused of idealism. When he heard about divisions and quarrels among Christians at Corinth, Paul was the first to ask, "Has Christ been divided?"(1 Cor 1:13). When he learned that the Galatian church was ripped apart by rivalry between Jewish and Gentile Christians, Paul chided the Galatians for forgetting mercy and then invited them to reside in freedom regardless of their cultural differences. Paul believed freedom was "summed up in a single commandment, 'You shall love your neighbor as yourself'" (Gal 5:13).

The Bible is clear-eyed about the walls that divide humans. Religious differences are no exception. How we approach religious difference may be guided by three theological themes.

Jesus sends followers to make disciples of all nations. Disciples are made when the gospel is proclaimed in words and deeds of neighbor love.

We preach Christ and not ourselves which means that indigenization without syncretism is not only possible but desired. Christians carry a message to the world—the good news of God in Jesus Christ. Our boast is the *Message*, not the messenger.

Proclaiming the message of Christ does not make Christians ignorant of social and political realities. While Christian faith took root in the soil of imperial rule, human slavery, and patriarchy, that does not mean that Christian faith is consistent with imperialism, human slavery, patriarchy, or other practices that betray the royal law of neighbor love. Christians are called to choose the way of Christ.

Christians, whether in conversation with Judaism, Islam, or other respected world-wide faiths should not only follow the royal law of love but should also heed a warning of the Apostle Paul. In his letter to the church at Rome, Paul compared Christians to a graft on an olive tree. In his metaphor, the children of Abraham were the root of the olive tree—the church was a graft. Paul advised the church, "Do not become proud, but stand in awe. For if God did not spare the natural branches, perhaps he will not spare you. Note the kindness and severity of God; severity toward those who have fallen, but God's kindness toward you, provided you continue in his kindness; otherwise you also will be cut off" (Rom 11:20–22). Triumphalism has no place in the church. Followers of the crucified and risen Lord live as a consequence of God's kindness. We "continue in kindness" when we welcome and work with people of differing faith and goodwill. Our aim should be cooperation with and mutual recognition of those whose faith differs from our own, not competition or condemnation. Judgement belongs to God and not to us.

INSPIRED

I will put my law within them, and I will write it on their hearts; and I will be their God, and they shall be my people . . . for they shall all know me, from the least of them to the greatest, says the LORD; for I will forgive their iniquity, and remember their sin no more.
—Jer 31:33–34

Hearts are changed by the fellowship of the Father, Son, and Holy Spirit. Jeremiah expressed this fellowship as knowledge of God written on human hearts. Hearts are inscribed by God where mercy and forgiveness rule. A million enacted laws cannot change one human heart. Hearts are changed by the Spirit of God.

In 1982 the US Justice Department launched an effort to answer a simple question: How many criminal laws are contained in the fifty-one-volume *United States Code*? The department tallied some three thousand criminal offenses. After combing through twenty-three thousand pages in the most exhaustive undertaking of its kind the project director concluded that a person could die and be resurrected three times and still not answer the question.[3]

Law serves a vital function. It orders human life. But, as the proliferation of federal law illustrates—and the example could be multiplied many times over by including state and local laws, together with rules and policies and regulations—humans cleverly find ways around law. Paul analyzed the conundrum this way, "[I]f a law had been given that could make alive, then righteousness would indeed come through the law" (Gal 3:21).

Law cannot make us do justice and love kindness. Not even God's law can make us *alive*. Like Cain, we never master sin apart from God's intervention. Despite our best efforts and deepest sincerity, we are captives of sin. We need to be made alive. We need to be set free. God's law must be written on our hearts.

Being made alive, having the law written on our hearts and being set free to love neighbors, is the work of God's Spirit. Creative justice is an act of resurrection and new creation. In Paul's words, "If the Spirit of him who raised Jesus from the dead dwells in you, he who raised Christ from the dead will give life to your mortal bodies also through the Spirit that dwells in you" (Rom 8:11). Or, as Paul wrote to the Corinthians, "If anyone is in Christ, there is a new creation: everything old has passed away; see, everything has become new!" (2 Cor 5:17). The Spirit frees us from slavery to sin so that we may love neighbors justly.

The Fourth Gospel understands freedom from slavery as abiding in the fellowship of the Father, Son, and Holy Spirit. Neighbor love comes alive when God makes his home with us. "Those who love me," Jesus said, "will keep my word, and my Father will love them, and we will come to them and make our home with them" (John 14:23). Loving God results in loving neighbors. Loving neighbors results in loving God. Disciples are sustained by abiding in love. According to John, it was Jesus' final prayer before his arrest.

> As you, Father are in me and I am in you, may they also be in us, so that the world may believe that you have sent me. The glory that you have given me I have given them, so that they may be one, as we are one, I in them and you in me, that they

---

3. Rahman, "Frequent Reference Question."

> may become completely one, so that the world may know that you have sent me and have loved them even as you have loved me. (John 17:21–23)

Neighbor love, grounded in the fellowship of the Trinity, is sustained not only by love but also through prayer. When we pray we are not alone. Paul writes, "When we cry, 'Abba! Father!' it is that very Spirit bearing witness with our spirit that we are children of God . . ." (Rom 8:16). Hearts are changed by fellowship with the Spirit in prayer.

God's inexhaustible kindness makes all things possible. Kindness draws us near others. Kindness summons us to kneel by the roadside. Mercy lights our path as we will see in the next chapter when we explore the meaning of prayer inspired by the One who provides for those who look around and embrace the world with the dawn of first light.

Chapter 14

What Is Prayer?

PRAYER AND PROVIDENCE

Whoever has seen me has seen the Father. —John 14:9

Do prayers cause God to act? Is that what we mean when we say that God *answers* prayer? Should we understand prayer as a cause? And if that is the case, does it matter how we pray? Should we sit, stand, or kneel? Hands folded or palms faced upward? Eyes wide open or squeezed tightly closed? Should we pray aloud or silently? Should we pray alone or with others? Should we schedule prayers or pray when the mood strikes? Does attitude count—sincerity, ardor, childlike trust? How about numbers? If prayer is a cause—do more prayers yield better, greater results?

Jesus taught his disciples to pray daily for God's kingdom to come and for God's will to be done. Does praying cause God's kingdom to come? Does praying cause God's will to be done? Should we think in terms of cause and effect—prayer causes God to act? Perhaps a thought experiment will help.

Imagine the cosmos without us. Consider a time when there was no us. Imagine a time 4.5 billion years ago when Theia collided with Gaia. *Theia* is a hypothesis, a Mars-sized twin of Earth, which may have crashed into *Gaia*, an early Earth hypothesis. Both are suggested by rocks collected during the lunar missions. The collision between Theia and Gaia may have produced the earth and its moon. Imagine that long-ago collision which knocked Gaia for a loop. If correct, the theory may explain how Earth has just enough tilt—23.5 degrees, more or less—to give Earth seasons in both hemispheres, which, with tides, thanks to the moon, makes for a dynamic living planet.

Imagine another just right moment sixty-six million years ago when a six-mile-wide asteroid traveling at forty thousand miles per hour smashed into Earth. The impact created the more than one-hundred-mile-wide Chicxulub Crater in the Gulf of Mexico and killed up to 80 percent of life on Earth, including most of the dinosaurs which had roamed Earth for 170 million years, which compared to the two-million year human saga is a very long run. The asteroid, which traveled who knows how many miles and escaped who knows how many other potential orbits, threaded a galactic needle. What were the chances? Then again, given that Earth spins at nearly one thousand miles per hour, what were the chances that the asteroid crashed just where it did? Had the asteroid arrived seconds earlier or several later we would be writing about a Big Splash in the deep ocean. Or, maybe we would not be writing at all; because, well, you get the idea.

Were these cosmic collisions accidents? Was Earth just lucky? Is that how we arrived—by coincidence, by good fortune? Let's agree that all of that happened— only it did not happen by chance. For purposes of this thought experiment, let's assume Earth is God's creation. If Earth is God's creation, how did God create without our help, without our prompting, without our prayers?

It sounds silly when put this coarsely but it may help us see that cause and effect is a poor way of framing prayer. That would be my take. I believe God answers prayer. I also believe we may experience silence when we pray and that some answers are *No*, but I do not believe prayer causes God to act. Prayer is not magic. Magic gives the illusion of control. Children think magically. They confuse cause and effect. Children do not cause parents to feed them. Children are fed because they are loved.

God wants us to grow up. And prayer is a primary way we grow up. Through prayer we surrender magical thinking. We learn to live by faith. Faith is not about getting God to do what we want. Faith teaches us to do what God wants. And that is anything but magic. Prayer puts our lives into God's hands. Prayer gives our lives over to the One who provides. Prayer is intimate conversation with God based on the benefits of providence. Both expressions are borrowed from John Calvin (1509–1563). Additionally, I want to consider practices of prayer or what Calvin termed *rules* of prayer. To begin, however, I want to clarify where I also part company with what some have called the "divine omnicausality" of Calvin's theology.[1] As Barth observed, Reformed perspectives regarding providence led to Stoic

---

1. Migliore, *Faith Seeking Understanding*, 108.

resignation and "the despair of frivolity" as a consequence of a "sinister deity" who ruled all things with an iron fist.[2] With Barth and many others in the Reformed tradition, I want to affirm that God "approves and recognizes and respects the autonomous actuality and therefore the autonomous activity" of humans.[3] As Barth states the matter, God "does not play the part of a tyrant . . ."[4] To the contrary, before all other things, God is love. God is sovereign, only not by his control of all things but through his love for all things. The full character and nature of God are revealed in Jesus Christ—"Whoever has seen me has seen the Father." At the heart of the universe stands the crucified God.

Because God is sovereign love, prayer is possible. Because God is sovereign love, we may give thanks in plenty; be patient in adversity; and live free from slavery to stoic resignation, nihilistic indifference, and other enslaving powers—nothing in all creation can separate us from the love of God in Christ Jesus (Rom 8:38–39). That is the sum of this chapter. Providence and prayer, like bone and marrow, are joined by the sovereign love of God. To illustrate further, I would like to tell a story.

On the morning my bride-to-be and I told my parents that we were getting married, my mother, typically calm and collected, pushed back from the table and ran out of the room. I did not know what to expect until she returned seconds later with a big smile and a small box. I've been saving this for years, she said, handing me the box. I want you to have it for Paula. It's the ring Billy gave me. My first reaction was relief. My second was joy. My third was curiosity: Who was Billy?

William David Halyburton Jr., a Canton, North Carolina, native and eldest of four, played basketball at New Hanover High School in Wilmington, North Carolina, where he was a member of the band, chemistry, debate, and Bible clubs. He also knew my parents. In fact, Billy dated my mother and lived across the street from my father and was his best friend. All three graduated from New Hanover in 1943. US involvement in World War Two was in full swing. Nearly 11 percent of the population or sixteen million Americans would ultimately serve.

Following graduation and with plans to become a Presbyterian minister, Billy enrolled in Davidson College and joined the Navy ROTC. After a brief stint at Davidson he was called to active duty. Because of his faith, Billy trained as a Navy corpsman. Sometime before he left for Davidson or not long thereafter, Billy proposed and my mother accepted. As a token of their

---

2. Barth, *Church Dogmatics* 3.3, 116.
3. Barth, *Church Dogmatics* 3.3, 92.
4. Barth, *Church Dogmatics* 3.3, 92.

engagement, he gave my mother a modest diamond ring. With Billy away in Maryland, my mother, meanwhile, began work in nursing.

After a year of training at the Hospital Corps School in Bainbridge where he advanced to pharmacist's mate second class, Billy was sent to Camp Pendleton in California to be readied for deployment. In December 1944, he shipped out with the Second Battalion Fifth Marines. His Marine group landed in Okinawa in April 1945. Six weeks later Billy's company engaged the enemy. During an ensuing firefight, a soldier fell some distance from the unit. To render aid, Billy ran across an open field of fire. Pinned by sniper, mortar, and machine gun fire, Billy laid his body over the Marine and was wounded. Though badly injured, Billy continued to assist other Marines until sustaining fatal wounds. Billy died on that Pacific island three months before his twenty-first birthday. For his "conspicuous gallantry and intrepidity at the risk of his life above and beyond the call to duty" William David Halyburton Jr. was posthumously awarded the Medal of Honor.[5]

Other honors followed Billy's death: a Naval Hospital at the Marine Corps Air Station in Cherry Point, North Carolina, bears his name, along with Navy quarters in Charleston, South Carolina, and Pensacola, Florida. Two streets were named after him, one in his hometown, and another in Bethesda, Maryland. A public park in Wilmington, North Carolina, was named for Billy along with a US frigate supported by a crew of two hundred. When my mother handed me "Billy's ring" I had no idea about any of this. She never once mentioned it. She held the ring for nearly thirty years without a word. My wife has worn the ring for forty-eight years. I imagine a grandchild will wear it someday.

My parents married in 1948. They were separated by my father's death in 1981. My mother died seven years later. After her death, my sisters and I were combing through a drawer of keepsakes when we came across a Bible that was given to my mother when she was a grieving twenty-year-old. The inscription read: *To Annette with dearest love in memory of Billy*. It was signed by Billy's aunt, *Margaret*. In addition to the Bible and the ring, my mother kept a silver hair clasp Billy had given her. Her name was engraved on one side. She kept the gift in a jewelry box on her dresser with the diamond engagement ring.

An estimated eighty million soldiers died in WWII. Eighty million is a statistic—Billy Halyburton is a name. With every name comes a story. There is a world of difference between a statistic and a name, which tells in part what I am trying to say about providence. God knows the name and story of every human being. God knew the name and story of each and every

---

5. Congressional Medal of Honor Society, "Halyburton, William David, Jr."

one of the eighty million who died in WWII. Their names are not lost, nor the name of any and all other human beings. Each and every one of us is known by God. Here is how Isaiah put it: "Can a woman forget her nursing child, or show no compassion for the child of her womb? Even these may forget, yet I will not forget you. See, I have inscribed you on the palms of my hands; you are continually before me" (Isa 49:15–16). The God to whom we pray and the God who provides is not an abstraction or an impersonal force or indifferent power. God has a name and God knows our name. We may forget God but God never forgets us. Nothing can separate us from God. We pray because God knows our name. And because God has given his name, we pray.

INTIMATE CONVERSATION

Abba, Father, for you all things are possible; remove this cup from me; yet, not what I want but what you want. —Mark 14:36

Abba was a name children used. Jesus called God, *Abba*. He also reminded parents that they would not give stones or snakes to their children if they asked for bread or fish. He then asked parents, "If you then, who are evil, know how to give good gifts to your children, how much more will your Father in heaven give good things to those who ask him!" (Matt 7:11). Elsewhere Jesus says that unless we "change and become like children" we "will never enter the kingdom of heaven" (Matt 18:2). The intimacy of a parent and child is integral to how Jesus defines our relationship with God. But when Jesus prays for God to "remove this cup" he is hardly being childish nor is he in a childish predicament.

Jesus had eaten a final meal with his followers during which he announced that they would desert him before sunrise. His arrest, trial, and death were imminent. Childish does not describe his situation or emotional state. Mark says he was "distressed and agitated." Jesus named his disposition as "deeply grieved, even to death" (Mark 14:33–34). By any measure that context and those terms do not fit childishness but they do disclose the depths of profound intimacy.

Paul, drawing on the same tradition, reserves the address "Abba, Father" for his portrayal of Christian prayer. In Romans, Paul's last known correspondence, he writes, "When we cry, 'Abba! Father!' it is that very Spirit bearing witness with our spirit that we are children of God, and if children, then heirs, heirs of God and joint heirs with Christ—if in fact, we suffer with him so that we may also be glorified with him" (Rom 15:17). Paul considered the *Abba* prayer as anything but childish. On the contrary, it is a poignant reminder to Christians that they "did not receive a spirit of slavery to fall back into fear, but a spirit of adoption" (Rom 8:14).

There is a world of difference between childishness and childlike confidence. Paul led anything but a quiet, reserved, contemplative life. Consider Paul's own account, granting that Paul calls his recollection foolish, however necessary to convince readers of his integrity.

> Five times I have received . . . the forty lashes minus one. Three times I was beaten with rods. Once I received a stoning. Three times I was shipwrecked; for a night and a day I was adrift at sea; on frequent journeys, in danger from rivers, danger from bandits . . . in toil and hardship, through many a sleepless night, hungry and thirsty, often without food, cold and naked. And besides other things, I am under daily pressure because of my anxiety for all of the churches. (2 Cor 11:21–28)

Intimate conversation with God does not lead to childish passivity. Prayer invites us to grow up and take responsibility. The poetry of Paul expressed it this way, "When I was a child, I spoke like a child, I thought like a child, I reasoned like a child; when I became an adult, I put an end to childish ways" (1Cor 13:11). Prayer faces us outward. It is not escape from reality but acceptance of reality, trusting that God holds all things together in his love.

Referring to God, notice what Jesus says in what would be among his final prayers: "for you all things are possible." Jesus does not doubt God's ability to control outcome. Jesus' focus, however, was not manipulation of God's control for his personal welfare. Jesus entrusted his life to God fully aware of the risk, a claim that was not lost on the Apostle Paul—"provided we suffer with him." That was Paul's caveat to prayer—suffering. Christians do not seek suffering. Suffering is not desirable. It does not win us points, but neither is it avoided, not if required by love's demands, which are never known in advance. We pray and live by faith, not by sight.

Prayer does not guarantee that things will go our way. Prayer is not magic fairy dust that if sprinkled just right makes bad things disappear or reveals silver linings behind dark clouds. Prayer does not resolve the mysteries of contingency or the riddles of stability, but prayer can lead us to hope for what we do not see. Prayer enables us to stand up and fight for what is right. Prayer gives us resolve to let go—to give our lives into God's hands. Those confidences come from what we have seen in the image of the invisible God revealed in Jesus Christ. We pray with assurance not because we have discerned convincing patterns in nature or observed promising trends in history, helpful though those observations may and can be. Singularly, we pray with assurance because light shines in the dark and the darkness has not overcome it (John 1:5). We pray because "the Word became flesh and lived among us, and we have seen his glory, the glory as of a father's only son, full of grace and truth" (John 1:14).

GRATITUDE, PATIENCE, FREEDOM

Do not worry about anything, but in everything by prayer and supplication with thanksgiving let your requests be made known to God. And the peace of God, which surpasses all understanding, will guard your hearts and your minds in Christ Jesus. —Phil 4:6–7

When Christians in southwest Germany looked for answers to mid-sixteenth-century conflicts they turned to two young Reformers who wrote a catechism. Most agree the principal author was a thirty-year-old named Zacharias Ursinus, educated at Luther's university in Wittenberg. Like most catechisms, Ursinus arranged what would become known as the *Heidelberg Catechism* according to questions and answers on the Ten Commandments, the Apostles' Creed, and the Lord's Prayer. Question twenty-eight of the catechism adopted in 1563 asks: "What advantage comes from acknowledging God's creation and providence?" The answer: "We learn that we are to be patient in adversity, grateful in the midst of blessing, and to trust our faithful God and Father for the future, assured that no creature shall separate us from his love, since all creatures are so completely in his hands that without his will they cannot even move."[6] While Ursinus did not cite Calvin, he clearly borrowed a page from Calvin's *Institutes on Christian Religion* first published in 1536. Commenting on the benefits of knowledge of God's providence, Calvin wrote, "Gratitude of mind for the favorable outcome of things, patience in adversity, and incredible freedom from worry about the future all necessarily follow upon this knowledge."[7] While Calvin and Ursinus do not cite the apostle, they would be the first to say Paul was their inspiration: "Do not worry about anything, but in everything by prayer and supplication with thanksgiving, let your requests be made known to God."

Rather than being swept away by cosmic insignificance and overwhelmed by impossible responsibility, prayer allows us to breathe, assured that life is God's gift. The cosmos is indifferent to us—God knows our name

---

6. Presbyterian Church (U.S.A.), *Book of Confessions*, 63.
7. Calvin, *Institutes*, 1.17.7.

and our story. Prayer does not eliminate striving or struggle or hardships, but through prayer we learn that we are not alone, not even when we pray. "The Spirit helps us in our weakness," Paul urges, "for we do not know how to pray as we ought, but that very Spirit intercedes with sighs too deep for words. And God, who searches the heart, knows what is the mind of the Spirit, because the Spirit intercedes for the saints according to the will of God" (Rom 8:26–27). When words will not and cannot suffice, we pray. By praying we surrender our will to God's sovereign love. We persevere not because we are lucky or strong or determined but because we are loved.

WHEN YOU PRAY

When you are praying, do not heap up empty phrases as the Gentiles do; for they think that they will be heard because of their many words. Do not be like them, for your Father knows what you need before you ask him. —Matt 6:7–8

Is there a right way to pray? If prayer was magical incantation, the answer would be *yes*. But since prayer is not magic "empty phrases" and "many words" are not required. Incantation seeks control. Prayer, like faith, seeks God and only what God can provide.

There are many forms of prayer: adoration, confession, thanksgiving, supplication. And there are many moods of prayer: praise and lament, feasting and famine, distress and relief. Prayer is encouraged at all times and in every circumstance. Whatever time, whatever mood, whatever form, prayer is governed by the character of God—"Whoever has seen me has seen the Father." Prayer is not founded upon a general concept of *father* or a widely accepted notion of *love*. Christians pray with assurance because God discloses his identity in Jesus Christ. Our Creator is our Redeemer. And our Redeemer calls us friends.

Everything that happens is not God's will. While we will return to this topic in chapter 19, it is important to repeat what was said earlier: we live in an imperfect world where God's desire is resisted and opposed. Prayer does not lessen opposition and resistance. Prayer makes both more obvious.

Consider the prayer Jesus taught his disciples. The first three petitions anticipate the completion of God's reign, the triumph of his will, and the hallowing of God's name. The second three petitions recognize that scarcity, sin, and trial remain contending powers facing every life. Karl Barth (1886–1968), a Swiss theologian and leader of resistance to Hitler's regime, named these contending powers "alien factors" or "nothingness."[8] Barth was persuaded that in the resurrection of Christ we see these powers defeated. As a consequence, we live with assurance when opposed by "alien factors." We also live knowing that we are partners with God in the world he is shaping.

Disciples are not just acted upon, we are actors. We do not just receive mercy, we show mercy. We do not just receive justice, we do justice. Prayer gathers us so that we are sent. Prayer calls us apart for Sabbath so that we are readied for work. Prayer is not just a means to an end. Like worship, prayer is an end in itself. Prayer is communion with God that draws us out of our-selves and beyond our resources. Prayer broadens vision, leading us to the horizon of God's glory. That vision begins with *we*. Even when praying alone, we pray in the fellowship of the Trinity. *We* pray in Jesus' name because Jesus prays with and for and alongside all of us. Prayer also forms a people, a topic for the next chapter, "Why Church?"

---

8. Barth, *Dogmatics* 3.3, 302–12.

Chapter 15

Why Church?

TREASURE IN CLAY JARS

But we have this treasure in clay jars, so that it may be made clear that this extraordinary power belongs to God and does not come from us. —2 Cor 4:7

Christians are estimated to number 2.5 billion people globally or roughly one in three. What connects them? How do they or how should they reflect the nature and character of the Trinity as the church? In answering this question I will follow tradition by first sketching the nature and character of the church as a means of salvation which I have titled, "Gathered to Be Sent." The second section will consider the marks or attributes of the church which I have titled, "Sent to Love." The chapter concludes with a section titled, "Traveling Lightly," which invites continued reflection on the irresolvable tension between the church as a human institution and God's new creation, which is where I also would like to begin—*this treasure in clay jars*. The treasure we carry is "the light of the knowledge of the glory of God in the face of Jesus Christ" (2 Cor 4:6). Those who carry this treasure are made of earth.

The reality is inescapable—the church is both an institution and God's new creation. Many North Americans hold a low opinion of the church. A 2018 Gallup survey recorded that only 20 percent of Americans place a *great deal* of confidence in the church. That number should give us pause especially in light of the fact that 50 percent of those surveyed indicated that religion was *very important* in their life, a percentage equal to those who answered that they were church members. More tellingly, according to the same survey, only three in ten church members reported that they had actually attended worship in the previous seven days.[1]

Given that nine in ten Americans say they believe in God or a God, these numbers are sobering. While sobering, they are not new. Colonial America is a prime example. In the late 1600s, less than one-third belonged to a church. By the time of the Revolutionary War, the number hovered around 15 percent.[2] Low confidence and participation in the church is not new. John Calvin, whose theological descendants number between seventy and ninety million, was depressed by the church. Writing nearly five hundred years ago at a time when we may imagine that confidence and church membership were higher, Calvin made this sobering confession: "Although the melancholy desolation which confronts us on every side may cry that no remnant of the church is left, let us know that Christ's death is fruitful, and that God miraculously keeps his church as in hiding places."[3]

"Melancholy desolation" did not lead Calvin to abandon the church. On the contrary, paraphrasing Cyprian, a third-century North African bishop, Calvin insisted that "for those to whom [God] is Father the church may also be Mother."[4] Fully aware of its clay feet but also emboldened by the fruitfulness of Christ, Calvin concluded that "it is always disastrous to leave the church."[5] Christ and the church belong together not only in Calvin's time but in our time, not only in a North American context but the world over.

When we are called by Christ, we are called into the church. The order of calling is not reversible. The church is created by Christ but Christ is not bound by the church. The church is a unique witness to the realm and reign of God's sovereign mercy, but it is not the sole or exclusive witness. The church may only give what it has received. Or, as Paul said, "we do not proclaim ourselves; we proclaim Jesus Christ as Lord" (2 Cor 4:5). Whenever the church forgets this, it ceases to be the church.

It is a constant temptation—substituting a human institution for God's new creation, a temptation endemic to church life. Christ is the end. Christ is the treasure. The church is a means. To further explore this relationship and in keeping with the center of Protestant tradition, I invite you to consider

1. Gallup, "Religion," poll 1690.
2. Fuller, *Spiritual but not Religious*, 13.
3. Calvin, *Institutes*, 4.1.2.
4. Calvin, *Institutes*, 4.1.1.
5. Calvin, *Institutes*, 4.1.4.

the church as a means of salvation under the signs of Word and Sacrament. To these I will add two other signs: fellowship and ministries of compassion.

GATHERED TO BE SENT

The gifts that he gave were that some would be apostles, some pastors and teachers, to equip the saints for the work of ministry, for the building up of the body of Christ, until all of us come to the unity of the faith and of the knowledge of God, to maturity, to the measure of the full stature of Christ. —Eph 4:11–13

As God's new creation the church does not have a mission; it is a mission. When the church folds inward upon itself, becoming exclusively a provider of member needs or when members seek the church only to have their needs met, the church is lost in narcissism. The church is gathered by God to be sent into the world. Gathering *equips* Christians to *build up* the body of Christ. Equipping may result in greater numbers, but it may not. The purpose of equipping is not a bigger church. The end is "knowledge of God" and "the full stature of Christ." The first means to that end is the Word of God. "Faith," as Paul writes, "comes from what is heard, and what is heard comes through the word of Christ" (Rom 10:17).

Language is a fundamental feature of being human. Some would argue the distinguishing feature. Regardless of form, God creates the church through preaching, teaching, conversation, storytelling, consolation, disputation, protest, resolution, and other forms of testimony. Traditionally, and especially within the Protestant tradition, preaching and teaching have been central. While proficiencies in biblical scholarship and communication are helpful, and while ordered ministries are desirable, the Holy Spirit writes the Word of God on human hearts. The Word of God is not bound by technique or expertise, which is not to say, that the church should not maintain high standards of scholarship and training; it should. However, the church should guard against undue reliance upon professional ministries of preaching and teaching. Ordered ministries are helpful but they do not create the people of God.

A single sermon may be preached to one hundred on Sunday, but one hundred sermons will be lived that week. The goal of preaching is not admiration of the preacher, but lived testimony to Christ by the people of God. When testimony is authentic it is not self-referring. It is not offered from on high but alongside fellow sinners. Testimony does not come in canned speech but through stammering words of freedom, freedom from self-righteousness and freedom to embrace others and to be embraced by God's redeeming love and justice.

The Word of God is not only heard, it is seen. As commonly defined, a sacrament is an outward sign of an inward and invisible grace. The term *sacrament* entered the Christian lexicon in the third century. While the definition remained fluid for centuries, it generally referred to the mysteries or *sacramentum* of worship practices, principally, though not exclusively, baptism and the Lord's Supper. By the thirteenth century, the Roman Catholic Church restricted the term to seven practices: baptism, confirmation, penance, Eucharist, holy orders, matrimony, and extreme unction. Citing biblical warrants, Protestant Reformers restricted the term further, reserving it exclusively for baptism and the Lord's Supper. In view of quasi-magical connotations, some Reformers dropped the designation altogether, preferring instead the language of ordinance. Still others, such as the Quakers, rejected any suggestion of sacramental rites.

The language of sacrament should be retained, not because it represents a mysterious change in water, bread, and wine, but because it invites participants to enter the unseen but real work of God. There is more to faith than meets the eye. There is more to faith than language can express. Reflecting on the Lord's Supper, Calvin expressed the inadequacy of language this way: "Although my mind can think beyond what my tongue can utter, yet even my mind is conquered and overwhelmed by the greatness of the thing. Therefore, nothing remains but to break forth in wonder at this mystery, which plainly neither the mind is able to conceive nor the tongue to express."[6]

The sacraments point us to the ineffable, but I also agree with Calvin and other Reformers who caution against sacramental practices or understandings which border on "magic incantation."[7] By faith and through the Holy Spirit writing the Word upon our hearts sacraments become signs of our salvation. While they are signs of salvation, sacraments are not necessary for salvation. I have worn a wedding band for over forty-five years. I like my gold ring and cannot imagine life without it, but I am not more married because of it. Baptism and the Lord's Supper do not make us more Christian but they do represent that we are bound to Christ by more than words can express.

No one is born a Christian. Christian faith is not genetically transmitted or transmissible. Christian faith is not a right of nationality or citizenship. It is not a marker of ethnicity, sexual or gender identity, class or

6. Calvin, *Institutes*, 4.17.15.

7. Calvin, *Institutes*, 4.17.15.

marital status, cultural heritage, or any other distinguishing symbol of our humanity. Christian faith expresses the new humanity God creates in Jesus Christ. Baptism signifies that we are newly made and united to God through the Son by the Holy Spirit. By this gracious work, we are brought into communion with the people of God. Baptism is a visible sign of God's gracious work of inclusion which is conferred by public declarations of repentance and faith in Christ as Lord. The baptism of infants testifies to the sovereignty of God's mercy, while the baptism of believers more closely reflects New Testament testimony to mercy received. Regardless of preferred practice, each signifies that because Christ died "once for all" (Heb 7:27). Baptism is a singular and unrepeatable assurance that we are children of God.

The water of baptism recalls not only the waters of creation, the flood, the exodus, and Jordan, but also the outpouring of God's Spirit on all flesh on Pentecost and the birth of the children of God by the Spirit, which like the wind "blows where it chooses" (John 3:8). Testifying to the God who freely creates and redeems, the World Council of Churches published a 1982 document titled *Baptism, Eucharist and Ministry*. The Council, a fellowship of nearly 600 million representing some 150 nations established in the wake of WWII, reached consensus on five principle meanings of baptism: (1) participation in Christ's death and resurrection, (2) conversion, pardoning, and cleansing, (3) the gift of the Spirit, (4) incorporation into the body of Christ, (5) the sign of God's reign.[8] Regardless of local emphasis, baptism signifies that God creates a global people known not by political or cultural identity but by faith in Jesus Christ. As Paul said two thousand years ago, "There is no longer Jew or Greek, there is no longer slave or free, there is no longer male and female; for all of you are one in Christ Jesus" (Gal 3:28).

Baptism commissions all believers into what Peter termed "a royal priesthood" (1 Pet 2:9). While some may be commissioned to particular ministries such as deacon, elder, pastor, missionary, and the like, and while for reasons of order churches will establish means of accountability and oversight, there is no higher or lower in the kingdom of God. There is one God and one Lord. We are called together to serve one another and the world for which Christ died and rose from the dead. Nowhere should this be more in evidence than when Christians gather each week at the table of the Lord.

The table of the Lord, also known as Holy Communion, Eucharist, the Breaking of Bread, and the Lord's Supper remembers with joy Christ's welcome of sinners; acknowledges with thanksgiving Christ's abundant presence in scarcity; and anticipates with hope the promise of his coming reign.

---

8. World Council of Churches, "Baptism, Eucharist and Ministry."

Jesus was roundly condemned by religious people as a "glutton and drunkard, a friend of tax collectors and sinners" (Matt 11:18). If we are known by the company we keep, Jesus was known for keeping company with sinners, the unclean, the despised, the rejected, the sick, and the unforgiven. While it is true that Jesus healed the sick, forgave sinners, and called all to repentance, and while it is also true that Jesus stands us on our feet and gives us a proud humility, it is always and everywhere equally true that Christ presides at the Table. It is the Lord's Table. We are invited guests.

We, who were once strangers and exiles to grace, are invited to the Table, which makes suspect Christian practices which exclude some from receiving and still others from presiding. Paul warns about eating and drinking from the Table "in an unworthy manner," but there are no warrants for restricting the Table only to the baptized or to those who have demonstrated worthiness. Paul cautions that we should *examine* ourselves and then eat. We should also eat with *discernment* (1 Cor 11:27–34). But there are no definitive biblical warrants for deterring anyone, male or female, from receiving or presiding. It is the Lord's Table, not ours.

What is true at Table is also true of fellowship. For a compelling analysis of early church practices, I commend Rodney Stark's 1996 book, *The Rise of Christianity*. If you have ever been dismissive of or doubted the importance of fellowship and ministries of compassion, read Stark's book. I conclude this section with two summary observations he makes. (1) The idea of a merciful God who requires mercy created open fellowship and ministries of compassion that changed the world. (2) Christian faith changed the world not by accommodation or relevancy, but by a counter-cultural lifestyle demonstrated by ordinary Christians.[9]

God's mercy changed followers and sent them into the world. If one parable epitomizes the church of the first three centuries and offers a model for being the church, it is the parable found in Matt 25:31–46 where Jesus says, "I was hungry and you gave me food, I was thirsty and you gave me something to drink, I was a stranger and you welcomed me, I was naked and you gave me clothing, I was sick and you took care of me, I was in prison and you visited me." When Christians embody this ethic in open fellowship and ministries of compassion they present Christ to the world. They also discover Christ present where they are sent. The people of God are gathered to be sent. And they are sent to love as God loves.

---

9. Stark, *The Rise of Christianity*, 209–15.

SENT TO LOVE

By this everyone will know that you are my disciples, if you have love for one another. —John 13:35

In 325 CE the Roman Emperor Constantine convened some three hundred bishops in Nicaea, a sleepy town southeast of his eventual imperial capital on the Bosporus. A dozen years earlier Constantine had decriminalized Christianity following his own formal conversion. The Emperor would not be baptized until his death in 337 CE. Regardless of his motive(s), Constantine's actions were at the very least ironic, given that Jesus' execution had been sanctioned by Rome three centuries earlier. The greater irony—and some would say tragedy—came a generation later when Theodosius declared Christianity Rome's official religion. While estimates vary, scholars generally agree that by the mid-fourth century Christians comprised one-half of the empire and enjoyed still larger majorities in Roman cities. At the time, the empire encompassed one-fifth of Earth's population.

In 381 CE, a year after the emperor's decree, the creed first adopted at Nicaea was amended to its present form and adopted. Today it is the most widely recognized creed among Christians. The third article of that creed, which bears great similarity to the equally ancient and widely used Apostles' Creed, includes four attributes which the fourth-century church agreed *marked* the church. The creed reads, "And we believe one holy catholic and apostolic Church."[10] Granting that creeds are not timeless but contextual and recognizing the political undercurrents and aspirations which undoubtedly influenced the Nicene Creed, these four attributes nonetheless remain useful. They describe characteristics of single churches which are attributes of the church everywhere.

Worldwide, Christians are divided among an estimated 1.313 billion Roman Catholics; 900 million Protestants, who are divided among historic and modern and Pentecostal Protestants; and 270 million Orthodox who are also divided.[11] How can we say the church is one? The only thing churches seem to have in common is division—is this what unites Christians? Even denominations are rocked by division, to say nothing of individual local congregations.

From the beginning, the church has been divided except for the name of Jesus Christ. Instead of wringing our hands over divisions we should acknowledge and even rejoice in God's wisdom of difference, recognizing that

---

10. Presbyterian Church (U.S.A.), *Book of Confessions*, 9.
11. Wikipedia, "List of Christian denominations."

God uses difference to achieve God's purpose. Jürgen Moltmann tellingly warns that freedom in Christ "can be destroyed through mania for uniformity, just as it can be killed by ruthless pluralism."[12] As he soundly advises, the church must return again and again to the "foundation of its unity in diversity, and to experience the open fellowship of Christ in his supper."[13] The church is one by virtue of its participation in God's love for the world.

The church is holy when it confesses sin and acknowledges the power of forgiveness. The church departs from holiness when it presumes moral superiority rather than reaching out in solidarity to the world which also labors under the weight of sin. Together with "the whole creation" (Rom 8:22), the church is holy when it longs for redemption by the mercy of God.

The church is catholic or universal when its love transcends the boundaries of nationality and cultural identity. No nation enjoys God's favored status. No tribe stands apart. The church is apostolic when its life is defined by love for the loveless and when its faith embodies hope for the godless and godforsaken. The church is one, holy, catholic, and apostolic when it loves as God loves the world.

TRAVELING LIGHTLY

Take nothing for your journey, no staff, nor bag, nor bread, nor money. —Luke 9:3

As the sun set on April 15, fire erupted in Notre Dame Cathedral. Hours later five hundred firefighters brought the blaze under control saving the main structure but not before the roof and towering spire collapsed into the nave below. One person was injured. Within two days one billion dollars had been committed to restore the historic Paris cathedral. Five days later, terrorists exploded bombs in three Sri Lanka churches during Easter Sunday worship and in two hotels. Three hundred were killed; five hundred were wounded. An internet search the following week disclosed a single relief effort totaling $76,033.

As Jesus approached Jerusalem for what would be his final visit, crowds shouted "Hosanna!" Some spread branches on the road, others their cloaks. Opponents shouted that Jesus should stop the display. Jesus told them, "I tell you, if these were silent, the stones would shout out." When Jesus saw the city he wept, saying, "If you, even you, had only recognized on this day

---

12. Moltmann, *The Church in the Power of the Spirit*, 343.
13. Moltmann, *The Church in the Power of the Spirit*, 343.

the things that make for peace!" (Luke 19:29–48). That same day Jesus went into the temple.

The first temple had been built on that site in the days of Solomon a thousand years earlier. It had been destroyed and rebuilt once and twice desecrated and rededicated. In the years before Jesus' birth, the temple was extensively renovated and enlarged by Herod the Great. Some stones weighed over one hundred tons. Walls were up to sixteen feet thick and reached nine stories high. Mark says that when Jesus entered the temple "he *looked around* at everything" but since it was late he retreated to the village of Bethany, a thirty-minute walk east of the city on the southeastern slope of the Mount of Olives.

Jesus spent the last days of his life in the temple. Controversies with temple leaders resulted in his arrest. Jesus is famously remembered for overturning the money changers' tables and driving out those who sold animals for sacrifice. That day Jesus cited the prophet Isaiah, "My house shall be called a house of prayer for all the nations—you have made it a den of robbers" (Matt 21:13). A separate incident sheds unsettling light not only on his prophetic actions that day but also his tears.

While in the temple Jesus causes a scene when he warns his disciples about the exploitive practices of clerics who like to "walk around in long robes" and love being greeted "with respect" when they are going about their business and how they must have the best seats in church and sit at the head table at banquets. Jesus not only accused clerics of praying "long prayers" for show but of "devouring widows' houses." It was time for the offering. Luke's artistic rendering bears hearing in detail: "[Jesus] looked up and saw rich people putting their gifts into the treasury; he also saw a poor widow put in two small copper coins. He said, 'Truly I tell you, this poor widow has put in more than all of them; for all of them have contributed out of their abundance, but she out of her poverty has put in all she had to live on'" (Luke 21:1–4).

While some spoke glowingly about the temple, admiring "how it was adorned with beautiful stones and gifts dedicated to God," Jesus interrupted their revelry with these disruptive words, "As for these things that you see, the days will come when not one stone will be left upon another; all will be thrown down" (Luke 21:6). Forty years later, during the Jewish revolt of 66–70 CE, Rome conquered the city and burned the temple to the ground. It has never been rebuilt.

What does Jesus think about the church's beautiful buildings? Is he proud of them? Is that what he wanted—stone monuments bearing his name? Was that his vision or is that our vision?

According to Luke, Jesus routinely worshipped at synagogues on the Sabbath. There is no evidence that he condemned that institutional expression of faith, so maybe his complaint was only against the Jerusalem temple. We cannot say with certainty what Jesus would think about institutional expressions of faith today. Jesus healed people; the church has built hospitals. Jesus taught people; the church has built academies, seminaries, and great universities. Jesus cast out demons; the church operates mental health clinics and sponsors wellness groups of all kinds. Jesus multiplied loaves and fish; the church runs food pantries, kitchens, and leads massively scaled world-wide relief and policy advocacy efforts. Jesus welcomed outcasts; the church has multiple ministries with migrants, refugees, orphans, and other displaced persons. Are all of these in vain—to say nothing of the explicit and implicit influence of Christ on humane efforts beyond those directly sponsored by the church whether by NGOs or government?

Like my ancestor in faith, John Calvin, I freely and sadly admit that we seek in vain a church "besmirched with no blemish."[14] I am equally persuaded with Calvin that lament does not excuse acceptance of the status quo, much less cynicism content with throwing stones. Because Christ does not give up on the church, neither can we.

Jesus taught us to travel lightly and promised to be with and go before the church to the ends of the earth. Peter had it right when he called us to Christ so that like "living stones" we might be built into a spiritual house (1 Pet 2:5). The church is a people called by Christ to embody God's love for one another and the world. Peter's words are a fitting place to end these reflections. While they do not resolve the tension between the church as an institution and God's new creation, they do lean us in the right direction: "You are a chosen race, a royal priesthood, a holy nation, God's own people, in order that you may proclaim the mighty acts of him who called you out of darkness into his marvelous light" (1 Pet 2:9). Worship is a primary way God's people bear witness to the light—a challenging topic for the chapter that follows.

---

14. Calvin, *Institutes*, 4.1.14.

Chapter 16

Why Worship?

LOYALTY

Again the devil took him to a very high mountain and showed him all the kingdoms of the world and their splendor; and he said to him, "All these I will give to you, if you will fall down and worship me." Jesus said to him, "Away with you, Satan! for it is written, 'Worship the Lord your God, and serve only him.'" —Matt 4:8–11

She was light on her feet and walked with purpose—a grandmother, I guessed—diminutive but sturdy. As I stepped onto the indoor track, she marched by and ahead of me, adjusting her earphones as she went. Six paces back, I heard her singing, *I'm not lucky. I am loved—Je-EE-zus.* If she thought anyone was listening, she didn't care, *I'm not lucky. I am loved—Je-EE-zus.*

Why worship? Because sometimes we can't help ourselves. Moses removed his shoes and hid his face. Miriam played a tambourine, dancing as she sang. Elijah sat mute, brooding in the aftermath of a storm's deafening silence. David wrote poetry. Solomon cited proverbs. Isaiah was undone. Simeon and Anna praised God for an unexpected birth. Wise men from the east knelt and paid homage, opening treasure chests to offer gifts. While her sister served, Mary sat quietly at the teacher's feet and simply listened. Startled and terrified disciples, disbelieving with joy, were lost in wonder when their friend showed them his once-pierced hands and feet. Paul prayed with mind and spirit and sang with mind and spirit. John, in the Spirit, heard a voice telling him to write what he saw, "I am the Alpha and the Omega . . . who is and who was and who is to come, the Almighty" (Rev 1:8).

Calvin believed that we cannot conceive of God "in his greatness without being immediately confronted by his majesty, and so compelled to worship him."[1] We are compelled to worship for many reasons. Worship makes some happy, fulfilled, alive. Worship builds family and community solidarity, national unity, ethnic identity. Worship gives life meaning and purpose and direction. For still others, worship promotes peace of mind, good health, and not least of all, prophetic courage. We worship for multiple reasons. We were created for worship. We are commanded to worship. We worship from force of habit. In this chapter I will consider a singular, principal reason—we worship because God is loyal. We worship because God keeps his promises. Because God is faithful, we worship. God's loyalty elicits loyalty. God's loyalty sustains our loyalty. When we worship we declare God's loyalty and our loyalty to God. Loyalty is born of God's love. We worship because God is love.

Before considering public worship in the concluding section titled "Last Day—First Day," I want to discuss two threats to worship. The first of these, spectacle, foreshadowed in chapter 10, will be more fully developed in the section titled "Truth." The second, entertainment, will be addressed under the heading, "Justice." While this essay does not have in view private worship, the theological issues are much the same. Additionally, because my aim is *why* we worship, I am not expressly concerned with *how* we worship. The two are connected and I will comment as necessary, but my primary interest is not worship styles. To begin I would like to return to the principal reason we worship—loyalty.

Fresh from his baptism by John in the river Jordan, Jesus was led by the Spirit into the wilderness where "he was tempted by the devil" (Matt 4:1). If baptism confirmed Jesus' identity as God's Beloved, the wilderness sojourn contested it. Such is Christian life. We are pulled first one way and then another. Scarcity, and sometimes abundance, ups the ante revealing what lies beneath.

Polling data consistently reveals that 40 percent have no religious affiliation. On any given Sunday, another 30–40 percent will be somewhere other than church. What should we make of these numbers? As we saw in the last chapter, these figures are well within historic norms so perhaps there is nothing to see here. And maybe that's just the point—for a vast majority, God is hardly worth an inconvenient hour on Sunday much less Paul's outrageous appeal that we should present our bodies as "a living sacrifice,

---

1. Calvin, *Institutes*, 2.8.1.

holy and acceptable to God" (Rom 12:1). What was Paul thinking? As Yale law professor Stephen Carter observed with dismay twenty-plus years ago, in our day, God is more likely seen "as a hobby" and is best left out of any serious conversation about matters of ultimate importance.[2]

Worship offers an alternative. Worship frees us or may free us from the soul-robbing wasteland of narcissistic post-modern nihilism. Worship delivers us from addiction to our next amusing distraction. Worship opens our eyes, turning us away from "the closed circle of our humanity" so that we embrace the light of the glory of God which shattered darkness on creation's first day.

It was not by accident that Jesus denounced the devil by citing Scripture regarding worship. All humans worship—the greater question is what or who we worship. When Jesus cites Deuteronomy, he declares allegiance to the obscure "little mountain God" of his ancestors who brought slaves out of Egypt.[3] The preface to the Ten Commandments makes it equally clear that the lawgiver has a name and is known by his works, "I am the LORD your God, who brought you out of the land of Egypt, out of the house of slavery."

Christians are not called to worship a general idea of God. Christians call on the name of the LORD or Yahweh, the name revealed to Moses by the burning bush, the name given to Jesus—*Yeshua*, "Yahweh Saves." Worship invites loyalty to this God and no other, the God who separated the light from the darkness and who gives life to the dead. Worship is a public declaration of exclusive loyalty to the God who liberates the oppressed. Worship has multiple purposes. The public declaration of our loyalty to the Creator who is Redeemer is among the greatest, if not the first. Worship is a counter-cultural act of defiance, a declaration of freedom. In worship, we give public allegiance to God alone. Competing loyalties are rendered secondary. Grounded in truth, worship frees us to embody God's desire.

TRUTH

You shall not make for yourself an idol, whether in the form of anything that is in heaven above, or that is on the earth beneath, or that is in the water under the earth. You shall not bow down to them or worship them.... —Exod 20:4

---

2. Carter, *The Culture of Disbelief*, 23–43.
3. Moltmann, *Sun of Righteousness, Arise!*, 121.

The "little mountain God" of Moses banned the making of idols. His brother, Aaron, had other ideas or the people did, "Come make gods for us . . . ." And that's just what Aaron did. Aaron took their gold, cast an image of a calf, and "the people rose early the next day" and they worshipped. They "offered burnt offerings and brought sacrifices of well-being" (Exod 32:1–6). They had a grand time. "The people sat down to eat and drink, and rose up to play" (Exod 32:6 KJV). Of course we know better now. EFTs make offerings a breeze. And besides, who has time, and why go to all that fuss and bother to dress and drive to church, when you can worship watching TV or pop in your earbuds and catch the latest podcast on a Monday commute?

Mass marketing came into its own in the 1920s. Among early joiners were tobacco giants peddling the virtues of nicotine, its health benefits, and most importantly—image. I was born in 1953. If researchers are correct, by my fortieth birthday, I had watched one million commercials. Now that I am cashing social security checks, I have watched a million more.[4] If Neil Postman, among many others, is right, thanks to pervasive electronic imaging—and bear in mind that Postman wrote before the invasion of the internet—our capacity for critical thought is even more compromised than it was in Brother Aaron's day. Should we worry? Yes.

Founders of American democracy were proudly convinced that truth was *self-evident*. With the Apostle Paul, they assumed, as most do, that "what can be known about God is plain" because God has shown "his eternal power and nature" through "the things he has made" (Rom 1:19–20). If that was the end of the matter we might conclude that a nature walk will do since the truth about God is everywhere apparent, accessible, and unassailable. Why should we worry about seeking theological discernment through worship, especially if religious truth is a matter of private, individual opinion? Is religious truth not simply guesswork, a projection of our deepest desires, longings, and dreams? When it comes right down to it, is not one image of God just as truthful as another? Why get too worked up over truth? Will worship lead us to truth? Does truth matter?

Ask survivors of the Jewish Holocaust if truth matters. Ask grandchildren of Mississippi sharecroppers if truth matters. Ask veterans of Vietnam and their descendants if truth matters. Ask mothers in Flint, Michigan, if truth matters. Ask coal miners in West Virginia if truth matters. Ask yourself when you look in the mirror.

How we understand God matters. And, in this age of spectacle, truth has never mattered more. The stakes are higher now because spectacle threatens to replace understanding. Electronic media, which couples

---

4. Postman, *Amusing Ourselves to Death*, 126.

flickering light with fifteen-second soundbites, has not made us smarter or safer or more secure. We are more insecure and more at risk because we have never been more susceptible to manipulation than we are today.

Eighty percent of our decision making is made by our gut, which was helpful when we were chased by lions, but it is a terrible way for choosing transportation or toothpaste, much less electing presidents—but that's how we do it. The cure? Cut the cord—worship. The obscure "little mountain God" was revealed through words and by the Word made flesh. Truth is discovered through worship.

Images joined with slogans do not equal discernment. And in this media age discernment has never been more difficult. In Postman's words, the union of photography and telegraphy has "denied interconnectedness, proceeded without context, argued for the irrelevance of history, explained nothing, and offered fascination in the place of complexity and coherence."[5] If a golden calf could dazzle and distract and distort truth, imagine what pixels can do traveling at the speed of light—especially in the half-light of a sanctuary. Disciples travel at a different pace and by other means—"If you continue in my word, you are truly my disciples; and you will know the truth, and the truth will make you free." In an age dominated by spectacle, understanding has never mattered more. Worship sponsors critical thinking about truth. In worship we meet the God of truth.

JUSTICE

You shall not make wrongful use of the name of the LORD your God, for the LORD will not acquit anyone who misuses his name.
—Exod 20:7

According to the third commandment we take God's name in vain and misuse it or make wrongful use of it by separating our actions from what God desires. Worship becomes entertainment when it does not issue in justice. That does not mean that worship can never be entertaining or spectacular or aesthetically pleasing. Worship may be enchanting, wonderful, and beautiful; but if it does not lead to truth-filled living it is not worship.

"One thing I asked of the LORD," David sings, "that will I seek after: to live in the house of the LORD all the days of my life, to behold the beauty of the LORD, and to inquire in his temple" (Ps 27:4). David seeks "to behold the beauty of the LORD." Worship should move us beyond ourselves and toward God, who in turn moves us toward his creation. When that direction

---

5. Postman, *Amusing Ourselves to Death*, 126.

is arrested by performance or audience delight, worship becomes mere entertainment. If the church is a means of salvation, worship is its end. But worship is only an end when it brings glory to God. And God is glorified where there is truth. And where truth is coupled with love there is justice.

So, does it matter how we worship? Is one style preferred over another? Is one inherently better than another? Not according to Amos who may be a strange bird for liturgical guidance. But given our amusement-driven, electronic-media-ravaged culture, which is short on truth and high on entertainment, Amos' prophetic word, however stinging and soul-wrenching, is sorely needed. Regardless of style, when divorced from justice, worship offends God: "I hate, I despise your festivals, and I take no delight in your solemn assemblies.... Take away from me the noise of your songs; I will not listen to the melody of your harps. But let justice roll down like waters, and righteousness like an ever-flowing stream" (Amos 5:21–24). Worship is not about style. Worship is not about *solemn assemblies* or *festivals* but loyalty inspired by God which issues in justice. Calvin could not agree more, "apart from the fear of God men do not preserve equity and love among themselves. Therefore we call the worship of God the beginning and foundation of righteousness."[6]

Dominic Johnson, who received a DPhil from Oxford in evolutionary biology, and a PhD from Geneva in political science, argues that "religion is not an alternative to evolution, it is a *product* of evolution."[7] While there are dissenting voices among scientists (notable among them John Wathey[8]) Johnson argues that, "[n]ew work in anthropology, psychology, and evolutionary biology suggests that not only do religious beliefs and practices bring important advantages in today's world (such as promoting cooperation and collective action), but that they were actually *favored* by Darwinian natural selection because they improved the survival and reproductive success of believers in our ancestral past."[9] Johnson's scientific thesis (nor Wathey's), does not prove or disprove the existence of God, but rather marshals evidence for the workings of our brains.[10] That said, at the very least we may conclude that worship, adaptive strategy or not, aids human understanding.

We worship because God keeps watch over his creation. God's watch is not surveillance, but a shepherd's care. The God who watches over creation delights in our worship when worship holds us fast to the fellowship of his

---

6. Calvin, *Institutes*, 2.8.11.
7. Johnson, *God Is Watching You*, 11.
8. Wathey, *The Illusion of God's Presence*, 15–18.
9. Johnson, *God Is Watching You*, 11.
10. Johnson, *God Is Watching You*, 9.

love. To paraphrase Paul, absent love, worship becomes a noisy gong or a clanging cymbal and we gain nothing (1 Cor 13:1). When joined to God's loving-justice, worship honors God's name, and leads us to do God's will.

LAST DAY—FIRST DAY

Remember the sabbath day, and keep it holy. Six days you shall labor and do all your work. But the seventh day is a sabbath to the LORD your God; you shall not do any work—you, your son or your daughter, your male or female slave, your livestock, or the alien resident in your towns. For in six days the LORD made heaven and earth, the sea, and all that is in them, but rested the seventh day; therefore the LORD blessed the sabbath day and consecrated it. —Exod 20:8–11

After the Sabbath, as the first day of the week was dawning, Mary Magdalene, and the other Mary went to see the tomb. —Matt 28:1

On March 3, 312 CE, Constantine decreed a state day of rest on the day of the sun for judges and townspeople and all occupations. Prior to the emperor's decree, Christians had worshipped on the Lord's Day, which, by Jewish reckoning, was the first day of the week. Constantine's edict collapsed these once separate traditions creating Sunday. Among Christians, the Jewish Sabbath and the Lord's Day became one and the same. The decree resolved some problems but created others. Tensions remain to this day. Among them: is Sunday the last day of creation or the first day of new creation? Is Sunday a feast day of creation or redemption? Perhaps Sunday represents each or both together, a kind of pause, a breath, a sigh—creation anticipating completion when God will "be all in all" (1 Cor 15:28).

These questions are not easily resolved and perhaps they should simply stand as testimony to the in-between-ness experienced by those who worship. We live between the beginning and the end of redemption. The day we choose for worship reflects this tension. As a practical matter, and respecting historical and theological claims and convictions, some suggest that Christians are best served by observing the Sabbath on Saturday evening and the Lord's Day on Sunday morning.[11] Already, within the New Testament era, Christians struggled with this issue or one like it. Paul references it this way: "Some judge one day to be better than another, while others judge all days to be alike" (Rom 14:5). Whether the issue was the

---

11. Moltmann, *God in Creation*, 296.

Sabbath or the Lord's Day or a day of fasting or perhaps feasting is a matter of debate. Paul's conclusion is more certain: whatever day Christians observe, they should "observe it in honor of the Lord" (Rom 14:6). With that in mind, I would make the following observations.

Public worship is more than a break from work. The creation story says that on the seventh day God *finished* his work. What exactly did God do? "God blessed the seventh day and hallowed it" (Gen 2:3). Blessing and hallowing are peculiar finishing touches. We are more at home with going and doing, with producing and intervening. As creatures of utility, hallowing and blessing are strange to us. The former makes us anxious, the latter makes us listless. Sabbath intends neither. Sabbath testifies to the given-ness of creation, deliverance of the enslaved, and justification of sinners not by works but by grace. As the first day of new creation, the Lord's Day extends Sabbath blessing and hallowing. On Sunday, the Lord's Day, the day of resurrection, we worship the Creator who is Redeemer, the Lord who blesses and hallows all of our days.

Secondly, while Jesus made all days holy and while he calls individuals to holiness, Jesus did not abolish weekly public worship. From the beginning, Christians gathered one day a week to pray and sing and break bread in conversation with one another under the guidance of Scripture. When Christ calls us to follow, he creates a people. Christians need other Christians nowhere more so than together in worship. Hebrews, a general letter to several churches perhaps occasioned and read on a day set aside for baptisms, includes this exhortation, "And let us consider how to provoke one another to love and good deeds, not neglecting to meet together, as is the habit of some, but encouraging one another, and all the more as you see the Day approaching" (Heb 10:26). Christians "neglecting to meet together" is not a recent problem. The habit of worship, crucial to discipleship, requires mutual accountability. While Jesus retreated to lonely places to pray, he also expected his followers to pray together.

While the habit of weekly worship forms disciples, it is not closed to strangers. The grace which welcomes Christians when they worship is the very grace which welcomes strangers. Christian faith fashions a unique grammar, but worship practices should not be so foreign as to be incomprehensible or unintelligible to the uninitiated. Worship does not take worshippers out of the world; worship transforms the world anticipating the world as it shall be in that day when there shall be "no temple in the city, for its temple is the Lord God the Almighty and the Lamb" (Rev 21:22). Worship, guided by truth and justice, serves this purpose when it honors God's loyalty to creation through our praise and thanksgiving. The next chapter will explore how work, no less than worship, may bring glory to God's name.

Chapter 17

Why Work?

DOMINION

God blessed them, and God said to them, "Be fruitful and multiply, and fill the earth and subdue it; and have dominion over the fish of the sea and over the birds of the air and over every living thing that moves on the earth." —Gen 1:28

Do you remember your first paying job? The summer I turned sixteen I worked for an orthopedist changing exam room bedsheets, removing plaster casts, escorting patients to X-ray, and making deposits at a bank down on Main Street (and yes, in those days, some patients paid by cash). When not in the office, I did yardwork for the doctor, cleaned his dog kennel, fed his horse, and shoveled its feedback—all for $1.25 an hour ($8.70 when adjusted for inflation). The following summer I worked maintenance in a cotton mill. I swept floors, collected trash, painted, and mowed grass—lots of fescue and no riding mower. Every other weekend, when the sprawling plant shut down for Sunday worship, my friend and I cleaned the mill's industrial air conditioning. Why we never contracted Legionnaire's Disease I will never know, but sliming out the water chiller and changing room-sized air filters got us out of church.

Before college I moved to construction—first pouring concrete and then swinging a hammer. During my last two years of college and newly married, I worked in women's fashion—inventory and distribution. The owner had five stores scattered statewide. My job was distributing and transferring merchandise, driving a 320-mile circuit two to three times a week. While in graduate school and before my first pastorate, I spent a year as a youth pastor in a suburban church. One summer I worked as camp counselor for children of low-income households. During another summer I was a chaplain at a large state-run mental hospital. For two other years, I worked as a counselor at a Catholic middle school.

When working those jobs, I never gave the meaning of work much thought. Some work was personally gratifying and some of it helped others, but it was largely a way of earning money—first pocket change and then, after marriage, paying monthly bills. Over forty years of ministry, I routinely wondered about the meaning of work and how vibrantly (or not) Sundays were connecting to workdays. Christianity, I imagined, was never intended to be a Sunday-only religion, especially when it came to work, where by God's design we expend a third or more of our time, energy, and influence. By theological training I was schooled to think that all vocations should glorify God or bring weight and honor to God's name. Work aimed to accomplish that purpose, not only by paying bills, but also by doing well to do good which meant that work was to be characterized by honesty, industry, innovation, and thrift. I still believe that to be true but in this chapter I want to shift the focus or broaden it in light of four worldwide and interconnected problems: overpopulation, unstainable rates of consumption, income inequality, and resource depletion.

The earth will go on without us but we cannot go on without Earth. Moreover, the well-being of each of us is connected to the well-being of all of us. And the well-being of all of us is connected to our number and rates of consumption. Ecology and economy are inseparably intertwined. Before considering their connections and concluding with a short reflection on work theocentrically imagined, I first want to parse the meaning of *subduing* the earth and exercising *dominion* over it.

Aided by crude stone tools and fire, our ancestors began to subdue the Earth 500,000 years ago. Two-hundred and fifty thousand years later, language accelerated our march. A cognitive leap seventy thousand years ago quickened that pace, but the advent of agriculture ten thousand years ago sent us into overdrive. With farming, we did not just add and subtract, we multiplied. Cultivation brought unfathomable possibilities . . . and peril.

From among 200,000 wild plant species, a few hundred were domesticated. Eighty percent of what we consume today comes from a dozen species, none domesticated in the previous five hundred years. Among 148 wild animal species, fourteen have been domesticated and predominate. Fueled by farming, our numbers soared from five million to 300 million by the time of Jesus. By 1800 CE population topped one billion, but as it turns out, we were just getting started. If farming sent us into overdrive, the Industrial Revolution kicked us into warp speed. Astonishingly and alarmingly our numbers have multiplied seven-fold in the last two hundred years. Even with a decreasing birth rate the UN projects Earth's population to reach 9.8 billion by 2050 CE and a staggering 11.2 billion by the end of this century.

Subduing is not new. It predates the Bible by many thousands of years. As previously noted, subduing makes humans, human. Humans do not simply live in nature—we transcend nature. We shape and bend nature. We harness it. We paint pictures of it. We sing about it. We cultivate it. We rearrange it. We tell stories about it. When God created humans he made us partners in shaping the world. The biblical story expresses this with the first command, "Fill the earth and subdue it . . ." (Gen 1:28). The command was not given to a particular people, but to all humans. The command signals God's gracious intention for creation. The command recognizes the status of all humans. All are made in God's image. Subduing is not the special province of Jews or Christians or a religious few. Subduing is God's gracious command to all humans. For far too long and for far too many subduing has been twisted into exploiting, expending, and defacing. I wish to reclaim subduing as gracious command.

Subduing, which includes work, creates culture. Subduing characterizes all humans. We are culture makers. And the cultures we make matter. All cultures do not equally promote human flourishing and well-being. Humans are also given dominion. Dominion, like subduing, has been warped. While God shares his rule with humans, all forms of ruling are not equally good. Ezekiel, a sixth-century-BCE Jewish prophet, offered this blistering critique of political dominion gone awry: "Ah, you shepherds of Israel who have been feeding yourselves with the wool, you slaughter the fatlings; but you do not feed the sheep. You have not strengthened the weak, you have not healed the sick, you have not bound up the injured, you have not brought back the strayed, you have not sought the lost, but with force and harshness you have ruled them" (Ezek 34:2b-40). Dominion, like subduing, should respect and perpetuate the givenness of creation providing protection, care, and benefit not for a few, but all.

Ezekiel's critique of human dominion was echoed by Jesus. Nearing the end of his ministry, and on the road to Jerusalem, Jesus announced for a third time that he would soon be handed over and crucified. Anticipating the arrival of God's rule and the benefits of God's dominion, James and John, two of Jesus' disciples, asked to become shareholders. Jesus warns that they do not know what they are asking. Other disciples overhear. A dispute erupts. After calming a jealousy-fueled shouting match, Jesus told the Twelve,

> You know that among the Gentiles those whom they recognize as their rulers lord it over them, and their great ones are tyrants over them. But it is not to become so among you; but whoever wishes to become great among you must be your servant, and whoever wishes to be first among you must be slave of all. For the Son of Man came not to be served but to serve, and to give his life a ransom for many. (Mark 10:41–45)

Dominion gone awry, no less than subduing gone awry, is not without consequence—not for others, or for the earth. Dominion which honors God does not grasp or take or exploit. Dominion which follows God's dominion serves and gives life.

TOIL, THORNS AND THISTLES

Cursed is the ground because of you; in toil you shall eat of it all the days of your life; thorns and thistles it shall bring forth for you.
—Gen 3:17

When humans began arriving in the American West fourteen thousand years ago they met a landscape resembling Africa's Serengeti Plains. They were greeted by herds of elephants and horses pursued by lions and cheetah. They found exotic species such as camels and giant ground sloths. Within a thousand years, most of those large species had been hunted into extinction.[1] Ten thousand years later, multiple descendant tribes of these first arrivers occupied the central Mississippi River area and in time built a city later known as Cahokia (Kuh-HOH-kee-uh). At its thirteenth-century peak, Cahokia, located five miles east of St. Louis, may have supported a population equal to or greater than London's, which then numbered some forty thousand. The people known today as Mississippians established trade extending as far north as the Great Lakes and south to the Gulf Coast. They traded in copper, Mill Creek chert (used for tool making), and whelk shells. Primary crops included maize, beans, and squash. While the Mississippians did not establish writing, the archeological record in pottery, wood, copper, and stone, along with an elaborately planned community, woodhenge, and multiple mounds used for a variety of purposes reveals a richly complex society.

---

1. Diamond, *Guns, Germs, and Steel*, 47.

Soon after its peak during the Medieval Warming Period, Cahokia's population sharply declined. Around 1300 CE, the site was abandoned. Recent studies marshal evidence that the site was repopulated in the 1500s and afterwards by migrating tribes of the Illinois Confederation, for whom the site would be eventually named.[2] Even so, the collapse coinciding with the beginning of the Little Ice Age demonstrates a profound connection between humans and the earth. The fact that later migrating tribes inhabited the once prosperous site does not suggest that deforestation, overhunting, disease induced by unhealthy waste disposal, and population density were not factors in the demise of predecessors. To the contrary, migrating tribes survived precisely because they lived within the limitations of land and climate.

The rise and fall of the Mississippians at Cahokia is one of many examples of the inter-relationship between ecology and economy. Dramatic others include the Indus or Harappan Civilization, the Maya, the Inca, and perhaps most famously of all—Polynesia's Easter Islanders, which by many counts is the clearest example of subduing and ruling gone awry.[3]

How humans interact with and manage the earth has always been difficult and was even more so for non-literate people who did not share the advantage of learning from the past. My purpose is not to pass judgment on non-literate societies for their environmental imprudence or to scold literate ones for exceptional environmental stupidity regarding resource depletion or bio-diversity regression. Rather, I want to echo a crucial testimony of Scripture which bears repeating here. The earth will go on without us, but we cannot go on without Earth. Genesis displays an acute awareness of the interconnections between economy and ecology. When those are separated or go awry, humans are alienated not only from God but from the earth itself. Mistrust fouls the ground from which we were taken, which produces thorns and thistles and compromises blessing wrested from Earth by our toil, sweat, and tears.

There is no returning to an Eden like that enjoyed by the Illinois Confederation. The question is: How shall we live? A major thesis of this book is that human life theocentrically imagined gives us a fighting chance to live well. Such a life considers the givenness of things and rather than cursing the dark gives thanks for the goodness of creation while walking toward light. Life so imagined does not collapse upon itself but finds roots and atmosphere in the life of God. It is directed toward the well-being of each and all, indeed of Earth itself.

2. Anwar, "New study debunks myth."
3. Diamond, *Collapse*, 79–119.

FREEDOM

You were bought with a price; do not become slaves of human masters. —1 Cor 7:23

Christians should not have one set of values and one allegiance on Sunday, and a second, separate ethic and allegiance come Monday. Following Christ leads to freedom—internally and externally, individually and socially, personally and institutionally, privately and publicly. When we follow Christ we are freed from human and other masters and freed for service to God. Scripture is keenly aware that economic systems can oppress human beings. Roman slavery was no exception. Despite advances over other ancient and modern expressions, Roman slavery was still slavery. Roman slaves, which in some reaches of the empire comprised 30 percent or more of the population, were not accorded citizenship. By law and custom, slaves were property. A majority not only suffered cruelties and brutality, they died exceptionally young.

Twenty-first-century economic practices, while not a moral equivalency of first-century Roman slavery, though in many quarters approaching it, pose a tremendous threat to human flourishing. The gap between the Haves and the Have-nots, not only within nations but between the First World and the Rest-of-the-World, when coupled with high rates of consumption and overpopulation, is a different form of slavery but no less threatening. The combination of income inequality together with high consumption and overpopulation is a toxic brew and has only grown more poisonous over the last two hundred years. How we subdue and rule these conjoined challenges, barring a K-T-like extinction event yields unimaginable consequence. We cannot afford to look the other way, blame, play the victim, or expect aliens to land tomorrow to solve problems we created. Though nations bear responsibility and reap rewards unequally, I want to consider all nations together.

Earth's inhabitants are split unequally between the Haves and the Have-nots. The Haves, numbering one billion, live mostly in North America, Europe, Japan, and Australia. The First World enjoys a consumption rate thirty-two times higher than the Have-nots. The Rest-of-the-World, numbering 6.5 billion, has consumption rates below thirty-two and trend mostly downward towards one. To consider the relationship between consumption, population, and available resources, Jared Diamond invites readers to imagine what Earth would be like if the Have-nots consumed at a rate equal to the Haves. If by a wave of a magic wand that happened, consumption would increase eleven-fold creating a world populated by nearly eighty billion.[4] That total is impossibly unstainable.

Diamond observes that some optimistically claim that Earth can support a population of 9.5 billion, which is just under the UN's mid-century projected total, but no one is "optimist and mad enough," as Diamond starkly states the matter, to believe Earth can support eighty billion people.[5] The path we are on is as reckless as it is dangerous. Whether or not we desire, plan, or choose it, something must change and already is—First World consumption rates are falling while rates in the Rest-of-the-World are rising. How far and how fast is the First World willing to go? Meanwhile, what will the Rest-of-the-World have to say about that? More likely, when will Earth cry, *ENOUGH!*

Thorns and thistles are pricking our heels, some would say our knees. The question is: How shall we subdue and rule the earth? Already we have cut down half of the Earth's forests and compromised once bountiful soils. We have exhausted many once plentiful open ocean fisheries, spoiled fresh water supplies, altered the climate, and blackened the air. The earth will go on without us, but we cannot go on without Earth. Unlike collapsed civilizations preceding us, will we learn from the past and anticipate the future? Will we exercise freedom while respecting creation's limits?

Anxious grasping like that condemned by Ezekiel and Jesus need not determine our destiny. More should be demanded of leaders, but we cannot simply wait for leaders. Many leaders count on our paralysis. Some feed and feed on our fears. Still others rely on cynicism or plain indifference, expecting that we are sufficiently amused and distracted while they laugh over drinks on their way to the bank. Clearly politicians want our vote, unless of course we surrender that too. Waiting on politicians and their corporate backers leads to more of the same. Rather than being overwhelmed by the enormity of our predicament or paralyzed by individual insignificance, God calls every one of us to exercise costly freedom which joins his work of making this world one of blessed and hallowed Sabbath.

How we subdue and rule by apportioning, cultivating, and safe-guarding Earth's limited resources will bring either bane or blessing. Until and unless we adequately address overpopulation, prodigious consumption, income inequalities, and resource depletion, our children and grandchildren and generations after them will never fully enjoy the fruits of labor, nor will we. The earth is home not just to the present generation, but also future generations. No one generation or any generation owns the air we breathe

---

4. Diamond, *Upheaval*, 141.
5. Diamond, *Upheaval*, 141.

or the water we drink. All generations share one Earth. The sooner more generations stop acting like Earth is inexhaustible, the sooner we will find green pastures and still waters so that this and future generations may flourish. Exercising freedom to subdue and rule Earth as God's good shepherds holds that promise.

CONSIDER THE LILIES

Consider the lilies of the field, how they grow; they neither toil nor spin, yet I tell you, even Solomon in all his glory was not clothed like one of these. —Matt 6:28

"Do not worry about your life, what you will eat.... Is not life more than food?" (Matt 6:25). I have sometimes wondered if Jesus lived in an alternate universe. Didn't Jesus understand that we must work to eat? Did he not understand that worry drives us to work and that if we do not work we will not eat? Even birds leave their nests. Even gloriously growing lilies stretch and turn toward the sun while sinking roots into the ground. What was Jesus thinking—"do not worry?"

The Sermon on the Mount is the most celebrated *sermon* Jesus preached. Curiously, the word *work* is never mentioned. Maybe the sermon is not so much about work as it is worry. Jesus didn't say, *Do not work*. He said, "Do not worry." Is it possible to work and not worry?

Most of us worry more when we cannot work or when work does not pay the bills or when work pays the bills but we worry that work might end or that we will lose our capacity for work. Until a generation ago, even in the First World and to this day in the Rest-of-the-World, retirement was a chimera. Most worked until death or died working. Given a longer view of history, retirement is brand new but increasingly, even for many in the First World, working until death is making a comeback.

Research supports the intuition that you and I are more satisfied when we work and when work pays fairly and is reasonably secure. We are less satisfied when work is unavailable or unreliable and pays unfairly. People are also happier and healthier when they find work meaningful and a source of dignified identity.[6]

Maybe Jesus was not speaking about work. Maybe he had in view the unemployed or the underemployed or those who *toil*. Is there a difference? Is there a difference between work and toil? Is toil different from work? Consider the psalmist: "It is in vain that you rise up early and go late to rest,

---

6. Pew Research Center, "How Americans view their jobs."

eating the bread of anxious toil; for he gives sleep to his beloved" (Ps 127:2). Does work become toil when we are anxious? Contemplate this observation: "Vanity of vanities! All is vanity. What do people gain from all the toil at which they toil under the sun?" (Eccl 1:2–3). Does work become toil when we have little to show for it? Might we conclude that work gone badly is toil? Might we conclude that work becomes toil when we are not just tired but weary, when we are not just frustrated but defeated, when routine becomes boredom or when pace and demand are no longer invigorating but deadening? Is that the difference between work and toil? And if it is, what can we do to prevent work from becoming toil? What can we do to keep work from becoming worry? More precisely, how might work be theocentrically imagined?

"Strive first for the kingdom of God and his righteousness," Jesus says, "and all these things [food and clothing and shelter] will be given to you as well" (Matt 6:33). The kingdom of God is both a realm and a rule. Striving for the kingdom turns us toward the world ruled by God. Faith gives roots and air for life in this world, including work. Work expresses faith that God created us for work and that work is good.

Striving for the kingdom does not spare us from hardship or disappointment or what otherwise may be named *toil*, but faith does bring healing and consolation and wisdom. Faith resists toil when our energy and attention and purpose are turned away from ourselves and directed toward God. We grow anxious to the extent and to the degree that we turn inward upon ourselves believing that God awards love based on good behavior, hard work, and doing all things well. Work becomes toil when we operate by a calculus of merit and reward. Righteousness is not earned but given. Likewise, work becomes toil when we are exploited and when we exploit. Work becomes toil when we *take* and are *taken*.

Exploitation is another word for being used, played, manipulated, plied, maneuvered, or capitalized. That last descriptor may suit best—exploitation turns people into property, into slaves. Exploitation is a form of commodification whereby people cease to be people and become producers or production units or the help whose value or worth is extrinsic and hence disposable. Commodification is the polar opposite of creation.

We are not the sum of our earnings or our net worth. We are not the sum of what we leave behind. Jesus says it far better: "Consider the lilies of the field and how they grow; they neither toil nor spin . . ." Before we are workers, we are God's work. Human dignity is derived not because we create value but because we are God's creation. No human master or institution can usurp or deny or destroy human dignity. We may squander and deny it and others may attempt to exploit it, but dignity is given and guaranteed by

God. Work theocentrically imagined has no other master. We honor God when we honor the work of his hands. In the chapter that follows we will consider how nations honor God by the work of making peace in the face of violence and upheaval through national and global efforts of subduing and ruling.

Chapter 18

God Before Country?

GOD AND CAESAR

Render therefore to Caesar the things that are Caesar's, and to God the things that are God's. —Matt 22:21 RSV

"I believe in God the Father Almighty . . ." "I pledge allegiance to the flag of the United States of America . . ." How are discipleship and citizenship related? Aside from nostalgic elementary school depictions of founding pilgrims and hazy high school civics, I have little memory of the formal subject. The early lessons I learned, I lived. Now, a lifetime later, I would like to share two.

On a cold February day in 1972, I sat with three college friends in a Volkswagen parked on a mountainside overlooking our campus. Posing nonchalance, we listened to a radio announcer call out Vietnam draft lottery numbers. I was an eighteen-year-old college freshman registered 1A. When my birthdate was the eighty-ninth number drawn, I told my friends that if drafted I was joining the Navy. My freshman year ended without fanfare or notice from the Selective Service. When my second year began I moved off campus. One of my three roommates was a newly discharged Vietnam veteran.

Harvey, 5'6" and 150 pounds soaking wet, was from a small town in eastern North Carolina. Harvey did not just join the Army; he was a Green Beret. Special Forces worked reconnaissance. Harvey was leading a team of five in the mountains of Vietnam when he stepped on a land mine. After reattaching his badly mangled foot, which Harvey described as facing backwards, the Army sent Harvey home with a monthly stipend and funding for college. Harvey's limp was not pronounced, but his scars went deep. We spent many late nights talking about the War, but what did we know about geo-politics much less church and state? Though Harvey had been raised Baptist and I Presbyterian, we were taught that good Christians were good citizens. And good citizens were good Christians. Citizenship and discipleship were of a piece. Soon after Christmas break that year the War ended. With the signing of the Paris Peace Accords, unlike Harvey, my youthful understanding of citizenship and discipleship remained untested.

My second story begins years earlier. In the tradition of previous presidents who honored Lincoln's birthday, President Dwight D. Eisenhower attended worship at New York Avenue Presbyterian Church on February 7, 1954. Inspired by the sermon he heard while sitting in Lincoln's pew that day, Eisenhower prevailed upon Michigan Congressman Charles Oakman to introduce a bill which Eisenhower would sign into law on June 14. The law added the phrase "under God" to the Pledge. A second national decision was made weeks earlier with even greater consequence. On May 17, the US Supreme Court ruled that segregated but equal schools were unconstitutional. A year following its *Brown v. Board of Education* ruling, the Court declared that schools had to desegregate with "all deliberate speed."

The elementary school where I pledged allegiance to the nation "under God" was located across the street from the church where I professed faith in "God the Father Almighty." For Wednesday afternoon choir practice, I walked from school to church without so much as a change of clothes much less attitude. To my youthful mind God and Country were co-equal authorities or so it seemed until 1965 when the Court's ten-year-old ruling took effect in my southern town. I may have been twelve, but I knew enough from what I overheard that the adults in my life did not like what the federal government was forcing them to do. Putting black kids in school with white kids who previously had not shared the same water fountains, much less bathrooms, was a bridge too far.

While I remained in public school along with the vast majority of my friends, some classmates disappeared to a newly created academy. My parents and their friends were law-abiding citizens. They did not protest desegregation. They did not attend meetings. And for the most part they did not say mean, nasty things, but they were uneasy. I did not have words for it at the time, but the closely woven fabric of church and state was tearing. If 1965 strained the cloth, 1968 shredded it. Space permits only a partial listing of that year's headlines.

- "North Korea Seizes USS Pueblo and its Crew of Eighty-two"
- "Tet Offensive Launched"
- "Memphis Sanitation Workers Strike"
- "Three South Carolina State Students Killed Protesting Segregation, Twenty-seven Wounded"
- "Martin Luther King Jr. Assassinated"
- "Rioting in One Hundred Cities following King's Death Leave Thirty-nine dead, 2,600 injured, and 26,000 Arrested"
- "Columbia University Students protest University Military Research: 1,000 Police Respond; 700 Arrests Made; 132 Students Injured and Twelve Police"
- "Fifty Thousand March on National Mall Protesting Segregation and Poverty"
- "Johnson Signs Nuclear Non-proliferation Treaty"
- "Cleveland Rioting Leaves Three Police and Three Rioters Dead"
- "First Special Olympics Held in Chicago"
- "Soviet Union Invades Czechoslovakia Halting Prague Spring"
- "Feminists Protest Miss America Pageant"
- "Yale Decides to Admit Female Undergraduates"
- "Shirley Chisholm First Black Woman Elected to U.S. House"
- "Robert Kennedy Assassinated"
- "Supreme Court Rules in Favor of Teaching Evolution in Public Schools"
- "Nixon Elected by 0.7 Percent of Popular Vote"
- "World's First Mouse and Word Processor Demonstrated"
- "Apollo 8 Manned Spacecraft Orbits Moon Releasing First Earthrise Photo"

How exactly was this supposed to work—this relationship between church and state? The year 1968 upended previously settled arrangements. It was confusing. By the time I was twenty, I had heard from church people that government knew best about killing yellow soldiers halfway around the world, but was dumber than dirt when it came to black children who lived sequestered across town. How was it okay for the state to send you to kill yellow people, but not okay for the state to send you to school with black people? What was a good Christian supposed to do? In church choir we sang that Jesus loved all the little children—"red and yellow, black and white, all are precious in his sight"—but that was hardly the message in the air or on the ground. Church and state issues today are no less divisive and puzzling. How should Christians respond?

"Render to Caesar the things that are Caesar's and to God the things that are God's." What belongs to Caesar and what belongs to God? To suggest a framework for considering church and state, I will explore three texts from the Bible. The first imagines a time of near anarchy in the days before Israel's first monarch. The second was voiced by a tiny Christian minority living largely anonymously in the days of the vast Roman Empire. The third was produced by the same minority laboring under growing Roman suspicion and occasional overt state oppression.

Thomas Hobbes famously named the state Leviathan, a metaphor first imagined in the mythology of Ugarit and Sumer. Leviathan resided in the sea, home of chaos. The myth, borrowed and modified by Jewish and Christian writers, was used in reference to state actors, most typically, monstrous ones. While I do not intend the term *Leviathan* in a strict Hobbesian sense, I will use it in a biblical sense as a metaphor for the state. After exploring biblical testimony, I will suggest propositions for thinking about church and state in a section titled *A Politics of Hope*. To begin, however, I will present a short case study.

RACHEL WEEPS FOR HER CHILDREN

Rachel is weeping for her children; and she refuses to be comforted for her children, because they are no more. —Jer 31:15

On December 14, 2012, a twenty-year-old armed with a military style semi-automatic assault rifle and a Glock 20 pistol entered Sandy Hook Elementary School in Newtown, Connecticut. He killed twenty children and six teachers. Before murdering the children and their teachers, the shooter killed his mother. Afterwards, he killed himself. Several weeks later I received a letter from a concerned member who requested that our church leaders take action by writing Congress to request a ban on the sale of assault style rifles. The correspondence noted that the rifle used by the Sandy Hook shooter was readily available and sold for $783. It held thirty rounds. The pistol sold for $577 and held up to fifteen rounds. The letter writer observed that legislation had been passed decades ago restricting duck and goose hunters to three rounds and it seemed reasonable that if we protect waterfowl we ought to safeguard people.

At the next regularly scheduled meeting, the letter was read to our congregational leaders. While leaders in my tradition do not represent districts or particular constituents, they do or should reflect a congregation's demographics. The body meeting to consider the assault rifle ban met that stipulation. Leaders were evenly divided between younger and older males and females, the majority with college and advanced degrees. While leaders in my tradition are sworn to uphold the church constitution, they are not bound in specific emerging issues. According to the governing principles of my tradition, leaders vote their conscience as they are led by the Spirit under the guidance of Scripture and church theological standards.[1]

I went into the meeting thinking that action on the letter would be routine. When the clerk read the request, the atmosphere ignited. Some wondered why we were considering the matter at all—it was a matter for private citizens, not the church. Others were offended. In fact, they owned the weapons in question. Did that make them any less Christian? Still others agreed with the request insisting that as church leaders we had a duty to voice opposition to the sale of weapons designed for military use. As a body, the leaders could not reach a consensus. After tense, though civil, debate, a compromise motion narrowly passed which urged individual members of the congregation to write Congress voicing their personal opinions. What would you have said in that meeting? What would you have proposed? How would you have voted?

How are citizenship and discipleship related? Does Leviathan oversee one realm and God another? Should churches worry about gun control, tax law, government spending, and other issues? What, if anything, should Christians do when claims by the state clash with claims of faith? Do Christians wear two hats—one for deciding state issues and another for deciding church issues? For guidance to these and other questions, consider three views of Leviathan. Each reflects a unique historical context and understanding of the state.

THREE VIEWS OF LEVIATHAN

Fear God. Honor the emperor. —1 Pet 2:17b

---

1. Presbyterian Church (U.S.A.), *Book of Order*, W-4.4003.

Leviathan, God's Ruler Reluctantly Conceded (1 Sam 8:1–22)

By the time of Saul, Israel's first king, ancient kings and kingdoms had been established for more than two thousand years. First Samuel, which tells the story of Israel's first monarch, who rose to power around 1000 BCE, was written during the exile by Jewish scholars collectively known as the Deuteronomist. The exile began in 587 BCE when the Babylonians conquered Israel, deposed its king, and deported leading citizens to the land between the Tigris and Euphrates. The Persian king, Cyrus, would free the Jews a generation later. The historical context for the composition of Samuel is important for many reasons, not the least of which is perspective—Jewish thinkers had plenty of exposure to the ways of kings before writing the story of their first monarch, imagined in a time of near anarchy. The back and forth between God and Samuel and Samuel and the elders of the people made a ready foil for disclosing the ways of kings and managing social order. The dramatic dialogue was informed by Israel's own four-hundred-year experiment and now collapsed kingdom and by Israel's centuries-long experience with kingdoms like Ugarit to the north, Egypt to the south, Sumer in the east, and Phoenicia in the west.

What is at stake in this story? Answers are given by three voices: the elders of the people, Samuel, and God. Justice and security are the presenting problem, which the elders believe will resolve if a king is given. The elders insist that they need a king who "may govern us and go out before us and fight our battles." The elders of the people want a king so they may be governed "like other nations."

Samuel, who once ruled the loosely woven tribal confederacy, resisted the solution even though he is aware that his newly appointed sons are taking bribes and cannot protect the security interests of the people. God, meanwhile, tells Samuel to give the people what they want. Samuel has not been rejected, God declares; God is the rejected one. Samuel may fear that the old order and his prestige are slipping away; God's worries run deeper. God fears not only rejection by his people but also their tragic re-enslavement. Before a final decision is rendered, God tells Samuel to "solemnly warn" the people by showing "them the ways of the kings who shall reign over them."

God's speech through Samuel is a telling depiction of Leviathan whose character and actions are captured by the verb *take*. Leviathan will *take* sons for his armies. He will *take* daughters for industries. He will *take* land for his farms. He will *take* private property for his work. And he will *take* assets for his retainers. Worst of all he will *take* freedom. "You shall be his slaves," God warns of Leviathan. "In that day you will cry out to me, but I will not answer you." According to the Deuteronomist, Leviathan *takes* freedom while promising justice and security which God alone provides.

After politely listening to God's stern warning, the people voice their decision, "No! we are determined to have a king over us, so that we also may be like other nations." Samuel conveys the verdict to the LORD and the LORD tells Samuel, "Set a king over them." And so it was. . . . God reluctantly conceded and Leviathan assumed the throne. His name was Saul.

Leviathan, God's Appointed Ruler (Rom 12:14—13:7)

During the reign of Caesar Augustus (31 BCE–14 CE) the Roman Empire may have included up to forty-five million people or 15 percent of Earth's estimated population. By the mid-first century, the city of Rome had an estimated population of 750,000 or higher. Jews living in the capital may have numbered as many as forty to fifty thousand.[2] Worldwide, Jewish and Gentile Christians likely numbered no more than fourteen hundred.[3] Christians were a tiny minority in the world's largest empire, an empire governed by birth, connections, wealth, and ruthless self-advancement. If those four factors influenced majority thinking, imagine the impact on a tiny minority which included the missionary and letter writer we know as St. Paul. Any accounting of his view of Leviathan must reckon with the singular fact of imperial might and ecclesial insignificance.

Paul wrote his letter to the fractional number of Christians in Rome around 56 CE. He expected to visit their house churches before traveling west to Spain. Paul eventually reached Rome, though not on the terms he expected. When he arrived some four years later he was under house arrest and likely remained so until his death. While Romans is generally regarded as his most developed and theologically mature letter, Paul's advice regarding Leviathan should not be regarded as a comprehensive argument. Paul does not develop anything approaching a doctrine of church and state. For example, he does not remotely consider the possibility of a Christian voice in political affairs much less a state that self-consciously or culturally imagines itself as *Christian*. He does not address the possibility or necessity of civil disobedience in view of an unjust or malevolent state or Christian participation in violent conflict between states. His thought does not anticipate modern republics or democracies or democratic republics. Perhaps most tellingly, Paul envisages that we are not long for this world which in his view is soon ending.

2. Dunn, *Romans 1–8*, xlvi.
3. Stark, *The Rise of Christianity*, 7.

Paul's take on Leviathan was not vastly different from a theology advanced by diaspora Judaism which had alternately suffered and thrived under oppressive regimes. In Paul's view, rulers, even oppressive authoritarian ones, govern by virtue of God's sovereignty. Because they are God's servants, rulers are accountable to God and deserve respect and honor. Paul, not unlike Hobbes after him, insisted that Leviathan executes wrath on wrongdoers and should also be feared. Moreover, taxes should be paid along with revenue.

Paul's advice to the Christian minority in Rome was pragmatic: Keep your head down and your nose clean. Engage the world, especially the lowly. Do not retreat or hide or live a cloistered life. Get along. You are not better than others. And do not repay evil for evil. If you have enemies, treat them with kindness. "Do not be overcome by evil, but overcome evil with good." Leave revenge to Leviathan, God's appointed ruler.

Leviathan, Satan's Provisional Ruler Allowed by God (Rev 12:18—13:10)

By the end of the first century Christians remained a tiny Roman minority numbering no more than eight thousand.[4] The book of Revelation or the Apocalypse of John reflects this status along with a heightened and growing acknowledgment of risk posed by Rome for Christians living within the vast empire. The Apocalypse unveils the power of Rome—beneath the gold and glory resides a beastly red dragon, God's ancient foe who resides in the sea, home of chaos. The dragon and the beast will ultimately be defeated and the sea will be "no more," John says. In the meantime, Christians should endure and remain faithful to the Lamb, even unto death, rather than worship the beastly red dragon—Leviathan.

By the time the Apocalypse reached its current form in the late first century, Christians had witnessed the destruction of Jerusalem and the temple, together with the death of hundreds of thousands of Jews and the displacement of tens of thousands more, John perhaps among them. They had experienced rising anti-Christian sentiment under Nero (54–69 CE) and Domitian (81–96 CE). Vesuvius had erupted burying Pompeii. Founding church leaders, including Paul, Peter, and James, were dead. Famines and epidemics had racked the empire on top of an ever-burgeoning threat, real and imagined, posed by the Parthians in the East. Whether or not originally composed under Nero or shortly after his suicide in 68 CE and edited or completed during or after Domitian, who extended and promoted

---

4. Stark, *The Rise of Christianity*, 7.

the cult of the emperor—three of the seven cities John writes had temples to Caesar—the Apocalypse discloses a cry of anguished peril from an oppressed minority and their testimony of hope for deliverance by a sovereign and loving God.

John's view of Leviathan is not vastly different from Luke who wrote during the mid-eighties of the first century. While the latter was likely a Gentile and the former a Palestinian Jew, both convey that Leviathan expresses Satan's power. In Luke's temptation story the devil shows Jesus "all the kingdoms of the world." The devil offers Jesus their glory and authority which had "been given over" to the devil to dispense as he pleased. There was but one catch, "Worship me." In good Jewish fashion, Jesus replied, "Worship the Lord your God, and serve only him" (Luke 4:8).

The dialogue reflects a nuance that may be lost if not named—Jewish-Christian thought expressed in Scripture, even in apocalyptic form, is never absolutely dualistic. John, like Luke and Paul, traces ultimate sovereignty to God. Leviathan may rise from the sea and may derive power from the dragon but its power is limited along with its time to prevail (Rev 13:5–8). John, exiled to Patmos, unmasks the tempting deception named and exposed by Samuel: How much freedom will the faithful surrender in order to possess justice and security? Will you sell your soul to the devil by giving allegiance to state or will you trust the Lord?

A POLITICS OF HOPE

We must obey God rather than human authority. —Acts 5:29

Christian faith does not have a singular, timeless view of church and state. Christian faith is contextual. Accordingly, the following propositions are intended to be illustrative and suggestive. Specific strategies and obligations cannot be known in advance. Faith is a lived response to ever changing circumstances, including our life as citizens. These propositions are advanced to assist faithful response.

1. God comes before country. Faith is prior to flag. If forced to choose, faith comes first.

2. Freedom is not free. Christian freedom is won by Christ. That freedom may be confused with justice and security promised by the state. Scripture alerts us to this Faustian bargain.

3. Chaos is real. Evil is real. Neither is co-equal to God. To address each, God provides for human well-being through the state. Christians

honor God by obeying state law, paying taxes, voting and participating in governance, including office holding and state employment, and by showing respect to those whom respect is due.

4. While the state may serve God's purposes, it is never our savior or master and may become our opponent.

5. Christian faith sacralizes human life and secularizes the state. The state does not validate or invalidate the church. The church acknowledges one Lord, Jesus Christ.

6. Christian faith exposes and opposes the myth of redemptive violence. While state monopoly of violence has reduced violence,[5] Christian faith overcomes evil with good. Even when seemingly justified, Christian faith has an uneasy alliance with state-sanctioned violence. In some circumstances, Christian faith may be opposed to state-sanctioned violence.

7. State-sanctioned violence may devolve into *just-violence*. Wisdom, vigilance, and witness are required to name, address, and overcome *just-violence*. Tyranny never conquers tyranny.

8. While all politics is local, we live in a globalized world. Learning to become global citizens in a localized world is among the greatest challenges earthlings face. Because Christian faith is not bound by ethnicity or flag, the testimony of the church may help humanity navigate this massively complex challenge.

9. All nations are under the rule of God. To equate any one nation exclusively and solely with the purposes of God is idolatrous. While states may secure many needs they do not and cannot secure all human need. To pretend or conclude or intend otherwise is idolatrous. Christians profess these and other limits on state power and dare to name idolatry when necessary.

10. Christian faith testifies to the creative justice of God which makes all things new. Discipleship and citizenship intersect with God's work of creation and redemption. Christ sends us as salt and light to live in, but not of the world. The church lives with courage and good hope when it anticipates God's final victory in Jesus Christ through daily engagement with the world, including the instrument of the state.

Christian faith connects every aspect of living with every other aspect of living. Faith is not a compartment, a day, an hour. Faith is not finished until the journey is complete as I trust the closing chapters will attest.

---

5. Pinker, *The Better Angels of Our Nature*, xxxvi.

Chapter 19

How Do I Know God's Will?

FLOURISHING

[W]e have not ceased praying for you and asking that you may be filled with the knowledge of God's will in all spiritual wisdom and understanding, so that you may lead lives worthy of the Lord, fully pleasing to him, as you bear fruit in every good work and as you grow in the knowledge of God. —Col 1:9–10

Nicholas Christakis, director of Yale University's Human Nature Lab, argues that friendship, written into our DNA by natural selection, "lays the foundation for morality," which in turn gives rise to "most human virtues . . ."[1] Natural selection, in Christakis's view, "provides us with something very profound: we can see ourselves as *all* being part of the same group, which means that, in the extreme, we can see that we are all human beings."[2]

Christakis's scientific conclusions on morality (shared by Johnson who views adaptive unconsciousness as "a sentry"[3]) echo portions of Paul's opening argument in his letter to the church at Rome. In making his case for moral accountability and consequently our need for grace, Paul reasons that Jews are accountable because God revealed his will in the law given to

---

1. Christakis, *Blueprint*, 238–39.
2. Christakis, *Blueprint*, xv.
3. Johnson, *God Is Watching You*, 30.

Moses on Mt. Sinai. Gentiles, meanwhile, "who do not possess the law" are no less accountable because they "do instinctively what the law requires." And Gentiles *instinctively* do what the law requires, because the intent of the law, given on the mountain, is "written on their hearts, to which their own conscience also bears witness" (Rom 2:14-15).

How do we know God's will? Do we know because it is carved into stone, or because it is written by natural selection into conscience or the unconscious mind, or because we know "instinctively" what God desires? I would answer this way: Christians know God's will by faith through friendship with God which leads to flourishing. We flourish when we are "filled with the knowledge of God's will" and "lead lives worthy of the Lord." Flourishing is the work of the Holy Spirit and it is life-long. Flourishing or living in conformity with God's will is also a function of character. And character is formed by practice, by striving and by letting go, by seeking daily to do God's will. Through the work of the Spirit we gain a heart of wisdom which not only leads us on "a level path" but bears good fruit for the world (Ps 90:12). Flourishing is transformative. By changing us, friendship with God newly makes the world, bringing "what is good and acceptable and perfect," namely, the will of God.

While informed by Christian thinking on sanctification, ethics, and spiritual formation, this chapter is driven by the framing question: How do I know God's will? My short answer of flourishing through friendship with God will be more fully developed in the sections titled "Character, Wisdom, and Discernment." Before doing that I want to revisit four aspects of creation introduced in chapter 11.

As we saw in chapter 11, creation is freighted with contingency, both moral and creaturely. By faith we seek to understand God in order to live faithfully in a contingent world. Notice the future tense of Paul's prayer quoted above and that Paul does not cease praying that the Colossians "*may be filled with knowledge of God's will.*" If knowledge of God's will was a *fait accompli* his prayer would be nonsense. As Paul says elsewhere, "we know only in part . . . we see in a mirror dimly . . ." (1 Cor 13:12). The contingent quality of creation together with the work of the Spirit suggests that God's will emerges. God's specific desire may become crystal clear in a moment but is never known in advance. We live by faith.

Imagine Shelia, a thirty-six-year-old, single mother of two. She is an hourly employee for a small town grocery. She suspects her supervisor is stealing from their employer. Her supervisor is the primary caregiver for his infirmed eighty-five-year-old mother who lives with him in his two-bedroom apartment. One morning over coffee with her supervisor, Shelia hints about her suspicions. The supervisor ends the conversation abruptly convincing Shelia that she will be fired if she reports her suspicions to the owner. What is God's will for Shelia?

After a career in public education, the last twenty as a principal, Greg retired. Four years into his retirement, Greg was diagnosed with stage four pancreatic cancer. Following eight months of treatment, including air travel and multiple overnight stays to receive treatment provided by a national cancer clinic, doctors tell Greg there is little more they can do other than offering an experimental trial. Greg and his wife, Alice, are nearing their fiftieth anniversary. Their two children and five grandchildren live in separate states. Greg worries about Alice. Their small savings will be compromised if Greg enters the trial. Greg loves his family. He wants to spend time with Alice and their grandchildren. What is God's will for Greg?

Life is unscripted which is why we pray for God's will to be revealed. It is also why we talk with companions—we need helpers. God's will emerges in conversation with others. Most of us know several dozen people well enough to pick up the phone and call. A handful of that number might be called in an emergency. One or two will know at least some of our great sorrows, our worries, our dreams. Knowledge of God's will does not emerge in isolation but in communion. Shelia talks to her grandmother. Greg phones a long-time friend in another state. Both find companionship helpful.

Companionship strengthens resolve while helping us identify our choices, which, given creaturely existence, are limited. Shelia does not have family money or savings to fall back on. If she loses her job, she may lose her home and her children. Shelia is a high school graduate and completed one semester at a community college before her second child was born, but her résumé extends few opportunities beyond her current employment. While Greg has Medicare and a supplemental policy, his savings are minimal. It is not just money that he worries about—if he enters the clinical trial he wonders if he will feel like seeing anyone. Will he be too sick to enjoy living and is that risk worth burning through life savings, leaving Alice more exposed? Greg's choices, like Shelia's, are limited. They are nonetheless choices both must make.

God respects and makes room for our agency. As we saw with the story of Cain and Abel, Cain faces a dangerous foe but he may master it. Neither Cain nor his descendants are fated. In another garden, Jesus faced a different reckoning. Luke described it in these words: "Then he withdrew from them about a stone's throw, knelt down, and prayed, 'Father if you are willing, remove this cup from me; yet not my will but yours be done'" (Luke 22:41–42). No less than Jesus, Shelia and Greg have finite agency. They are human.

We know God's will by faith through friendship with God. Faith does not remove every uncertainty. Faith does not erase all doubt. Faith does not make every decision right. But faith does commit our will to God trusting that in all things and in every circumstance God wills that which is "good and acceptable and perfect."

CHARACTER

Your will be done, on earth as it is in heaven. —Matt 6:10

Thousands of years ago using a reed stylus, scribes cut cuneiform or wedged shaped letters into soft clay tablets which were then baked dry in the sun. The word *character* derives from a word meaning *to cut*—character is cut into us. It is traced, inscribed. The things we do over and over again are etched into our souls, forming a large measure of our identity. Megan Rapinoe was not born knowing how to kick a soccer ball. Tiger Woods was not born with a nine iron in his hand. Had Beethoven been born to a blacksmith and not a music teacher, we likely would not even know his name. Great musicians and athletes alike are typically uniquely gifted, but as Thomas Edison famously observed, genius is 1 percent inspiration and 99 percent perspiration. Character, formed over a lifetime, is less about genius and more about practice. It was not by accident that Jesus taught his disciples to pray *daily*, "Your will be done on earth as it is in heaven." Friendship with God comes with practice, with repetition, with striving and seeking, and with letting go. Knowing God's will comes with character and character comes through practice and repeated exposure to classic expressions of God's will.

Reformed catechisms were typically framed by the Ten Commandments, the Apostles' Creed, and the Lord's Prayer. Catechesis was given prior to baptism or confirmation. While Reformed catechesis might be faulted for placing too much emphasis on the mind and too little on the heart and soul, the aim was right: shaping life in accord with God's will. Catechesis aims to form character and character building requires not only spiritual muscle memory but tools. Microscopes and telescopes are essential tools if you want to see cells and stars. We are not born with microscopic or telescopic vision. While we may be born with a DNA-scripted conscience or unconscious mind, neither, nor both together, are sufficient to navigate moral complexity. Habits of faith shaped by tradition equip us to see what was previously hidden and perhaps more importantly provide courage and endurance when the way is not clear or clear but seemingly impossible.

Paul, ever inventive and occasionally borrowing from and amending exemplars familiar to his readers, drew upon a suite of metaphors to mold and embolden disciples. Paul could speak to the Corinthians about *gifts* of the Spirit (1 Cor 12:1–11). He invited the Galatians to produce *fruits* of the Spirit (Gal 5:22–23). And to the Ephesians, he wrote of putting on the *armor* of God (Eph 6:10–17). With each metaphor, Paul aimed to advance his readers' moral ambition and conviction. Knowledge of God's will is not guesswork. It has many resources but is gained foremost by looking to Jesus Christ, "the image of the invisible God . . ." (Col 1:15). If we want to know the will of God, we look to Christ. By daily following the Messiah, his character is engraved on our hearts and minds and souls so that God's will may be done on earth as it is in heaven.

WISDOM

Teach me to do your will, for you are my God. Let your good spirit lead me on a level path. —Ps 143:10

According to the Fourth Gospel, when Jesus prepared his disciples for his death, he promised not to leave them orphaned. "In a little while the world will no longer see me, but you will see me," Jesus tells his disciples.

> On that day you will know that I am in my Father, and you in me, and I in you. . . . Those who love me will keep my word, and my Father will love them, and we will come and make our home with them. . . . I have said these to you while I am still with you. But the Advocate, the Holy Spirit, whom the Father will send in my name, will teach you everything, and remind you of all that I have said to you (John 14:18–26).

Friendship with God is not first an ethical system but communion with God. Friendship with God is not an arcane discipline reserved for a select few but is given in plain sight by the Spirit and is available to all. Jesus said it this way, "This is my commandment, that you love one another as I have loved you. No one has greater love than this, to lay down one's life for one's friends. You are my friends if you do what I command you. I do not call you servants any longer . . . but I have called you friends . . ." (John 15:12–15).

Friendship with God is possible because God reveals his love. In John's language we have seen God's love because "the Word became flesh and lived among us . . ." (John 1:14). The Word which became flesh was the Word which was in the beginning with God (John 1:1). Redemption begins with creation. Creation is not one act followed by a second act called redemption. Creation and redemption are distinguished but not separated. The "wind from God" which "swept over the face of the waters" (Gen 1:2) was the Word made flesh who promised the Advocate who would never leave disciples orphaned (John 14:15–31). The Old Testament names this Word, this Spirit—Wisdom.

According to Proverbs, "The LORD by wisdom founded the earth; by understanding he established the heaven; by his knowledge the deeps broke open . . ." (Prov 3:19). Proverbs invites listeners to call wisdom "intimate friend" (Prov 7:4). The most complete depiction of Wisdom is found in the eighth chapter, a portion of which reads,

> When he established the heavens, I was there, when he drew a circle on the face of the deep, when he made firm the skies above, when he established the foundations of the deep, when he assigned the sea its limit, so that the waters might not transgress his command, when he marked out the foundations of the earth, then I was beside him, like a master worker; and I was daily his delight, rejoicing before him always, rejoicing in his inhabited world and delighting in the human race" (Prov 8:27–31).

The imagery of Proverbs recalls and informs the kaleidoscopic Trinity introduced in the first chapter of this book. The Father who is up, above, and over us is also the Son who is with and for us no less than the Spirit who is before, in, and among us. To employ more traditional theological language, the God who justifies also sanctifies us.

Grace is newly given every morning so that we may grow up, mature, and walk on "a level path." Wisdom, given by the Spirit, is not simply a product of age or experience but a work of the One who delights in the human race. That work may begin at any age. We do not have to be old to be wise but we do need a teachable spirit. Curiosity, coupled with humility and a healthy dose of vulnerability, honesty, and a teachable spirit, are the makings of a wise heart. God wants us to grow firm in our convictions and in understanding. That kind of growth does not ossify hearts but makes them supple and open to the beauty and wonder of God. Growing up requires letting go. Wisdom lets go of the past and our need to control the future. Our times are in God's hands. The Spirit who is our beginning and our end gives us wisdom which sustains and newly creates us in all times.

DISCERNMENT

Do not be conformed to this world, but be transformed by the renewing of your minds, so that you may discern what is the will of God—what is good and acceptable and perfect. —Rom 12:2

What is God's will for Shelia? What is God's will for Greg? Must either or both simply choose between right and wrong, truth and error? Does truth demand that Shelia report her supervisor or does providing for her children require her silence? And if she tells the truth, what will happen to the supervisor's mother? If the supervisor's son goes to jail, who will care for his mother? How does Shelia discern God's will? Does Greg wager life savings on the possibility of extra months, perhaps many months? But if he has the treatment and is miserable, what has he gained? Should he forgo treatment, hoping to make the most of whatever good months remain? Should Greg do what is best for him? What is best for Alice? What about their children or grandchildren? Do they deserve consideration? How does Greg discern God's will?

In some instances discernment may be a matter of choosing between right and wrong, truth and error; but more times than not, life does not fit black and white categories. Paul expresses the nature of discernment when he invites us to work out our salvation with "fear and trembling" (Phil 2:12). Paul had in view something other than fretfulness. Help comes from God who works in us, enabling us "both to will and to work for his good pleasure" (Phil 2:13). God does not kick us out of the nest only to wish us good luck. God walks with us, before us, and behind us—always. That does not mean God simply endorses whatever conclusions we reach or paths we take. An easy equivalence between the voice inside our head and the voice of God can be dangerous, which is all the more reason why character and wisdom are necessary. Both help us avoid uncontested equivalency between our will and God's will. Jesus sweated blood in the garden. "Fear and trembling" are signs of discernment. Character and wisdom give way to grace—not our will but God's will be done.

Antiquity identified four cardinal virtues: prudence, courage, temperance, and justice. Christians freely borrowed and modified these traits, adding faith, hope, and love. Anxious to avoid any appearance of "works righteousness" Protestant Reformers closely tied justification and sanctification when referencing these and other virtues. Some avoided the idea of virtue altogether for fear that redemption by grace alone would disappear into redemption by faith alone. We do well to heed their warning. We never leave justification behind. Luther aptly reminds us that we are and remain simultaneously justified and sinners. Double red flags should be posted over these waters, especially in a North American context where self-determination and self-help are driving forces. That said, God does not do everything. Moreover, as noted in chapter 14, everything that happens is not God's will. If everything is God's will—what is to discern? If God does everything—why pray for God's will to be done? Discernment requires "fear and trembling" precisely because everything that happens is not God's will. "Fear and trembling" confounds arrogance, conceit, self-importance, superiority, self-aggrandizement, and self-pity. "Fear and trembling" represents seeking, yielding, asking, surrendering, and thinking critically and honestly. "Fear and trembling" provides a context for openness, vulnerability, courage, and perhaps most of all—hope.

Hearts tempered by "fear and trembling" are starched with resolve. Isaiah put it this way: "I have set my face like flint. . . . Who will contend with me? Let us stand up together. Let them confront me" (Isa 50:7–8). Luke echoed this resolve when describing Jesus' decision regarding Jerusalem, "When the days drew near for him to be taken up, he set his face to go to Jerusalem." Luke ends the episode with a proverb characterizing resolve, "No one who puts a hand to the plow and looks back is fit for the kingdom of God" (Luke 9:51–62).

"Fear and trembling" yields courage, confidence, persistence, and endurance. Ultimately, it also brings peace, the kind of peace "which surpasses all understanding," peace which guards our hearts and minds (Phil 4:7). Peace is not the absence of conflict or turmoil. While akin to calm beneath the storm, peace which surpasses understanding is funded by the inexhaustible love of God. Peace anchors the heart in the treasury of the cross and empty tomb, where we rest in the certainty of God's wisdom, not our cleverness. Peace abides in the forgiveness of sins, not the absence of regret. Peace which surpasses understanding is grace.

Greg did not enter the experimental trial. He and Alice took a road trip and watched the sun set from the edge of the Grand Canyon. Greg attended a Little League game and cheered when his grandson caught a fly ball in right field. He saw his granddaughter win a red ribbon at a state swim meet. He and his high school friend spoke every week. Greg lived five months.

Shelia kept her job at the grocery. Her supervisor confessed. On recommendation from the store owner, the judge suspended jail time in lieu of restitution and two years of probation. The supervisor's mother celebrated her eighty-sixth birthday. Shelia re-enrolled in school and graduated with an associate's degree in bookkeeping. She and her supervisor remain friends.

God desires human flourishing. Flourishing comes by faith through friendship with God who delights in his creation. He did from the first and will until the last, a topic for the next chapter.

Chapter 20

World Without End?

KEEP ALERT

But about that day or hour no one knows, neither the angels in heaven, nor the Son, but only the Father. Beware, keep alert; for you do not know when the time will come. —Mark 13:32–33

Imagine Earth a long time from now—not in thirty years when global population is expected to reach 9.8 billion or eighty years when it may top eleven billion. Imagine Earth in a thousand years. What will Earth be like in 3019? Contrary to Stephen Hawking's prediction, will humans survive? And if we survive, what will we be like? But don't stop there. Imagine Earth in ten thousand years when sea level rise is not two feet, as estimated by the end of this century, but ten to thirteen feet. What then? But don't stop there. Imagine Earth not in ten thousand years or even in fifty thousand when Niagara Falls has eroded and disappeared into Lake Erie—imagine Earth in two million years when the Grand Canyon is little more than a broad valley on either side of the Colorado River, but keep going. Imagine Earth when the Appalachian Mountains and the Canadian and Southern Rockies have become gently rolling hills while Africa has collided with Eurasia closing the Mediterranean Sea basin—imagine a time 250 million years from now when the Americas and Eurasia-Africa have merged with all other land masses, forming Pangaea Ultima.[1]

1. NASA, "Continents in Collision"

Mind-boggling, isn't it? We can hardly fathom a time ten thousand years from now much less 250 million, but even 250 million is not the end of Earth. Fast forward to a time when the sun begins its own death march and along the way destroys Earth's plant life 600 million years from now and virtually all other Earth life forms one billion years later. Add another billion years to that and Earth's oceans will be no more. But wait 7.9 billion years from now until that time when the sun reaches its red-giant maximum radius, and Earth too will be no more.[2] It will end. Can you imagine that? What does that time do to this time, this day, this now?

Every story has a beginning, a middle, and an end. We have come to the end of this one, this look around for a twenty-first-century Christian faith. What does the end hold—not just the end of each of us individually—but the end of us all and of Earth? And how does that end influence how we live here and now? Before attempting an answer, I am reminded not only of the limits of language but also of the necessity of humility. Waist deep in a thick discussion of immortality, Calvin reminded readers of both truths, observing that "it is foolish and rash to inquire concerning unknown matters more deeply than God permits us to know. Scripture goes no farther than to say that Christ is present with them, and receives them into paradise."[3] In keeping with Calvin, among many others, I will plead ignorance about matters unknown while venturing testimony that presses against and yet respects the limits of Scripture and its invitation to imagine. I aim to speak a word "through faith for faith" not only about judgment and new creation, but also hope. I first want to frame more precisely what I mean by the *end* of the world while commenting about an apocalyptic eschatology.

In chapter 2 we considered how origins mold identity. In this chapter we will investigate how destiny fashions identity. Where we are going is no less important than where we are from. Eschatology inquires about the end—traditionally, the meaning of death, judgment, eternal life, and the destiny of Earth. More generally, eschatology is a point of view, a way of seeing, a vantage from which we make sense of what appears. If creation theology sees life from its beginning, eschatology views life from its end. Apocalyptic eschatology is a particular kind of eschatology or way of thinking about the end. Apocalyptic eschatology is characterized by urgency and a largely or near binary outlook regarding good and evil; the righteous and the wicked; this age and the age to come; and, among other things, the nearness of redemption and God's passionate determination to achieve his purposes. An apocalyptic eschatology expects God to act soon and decisively to set

---

2. Wikipedia, "Timeline of the far future."
3. Calvin, *Institutes*, 3.25.6.

the world aright once and for all time. Versions of apocalyptic eschatology underlie much of the New Testament and not just the book of Revelation.[4]

Despite warnings, claims, and examples to the contrary, an apocalyptic eschatology does not necessarily and always lead to dystopian *Chicken Little* Christian escapism or to its secular twin, nihilism, whether of a stoical or hedonistic type. Moreover, an apocalyptic eschatology does not default to Christian or secular utopias. It leads, or it may lead, to radical hope in God's sovereign love in Jesus Christ which conquers all things making them new. God's new creation is the destiny of the world.

An apocalyptic eschatology makes and keeps us *alert* to God's redemptive work. It makes us driven, not afraid or frantic or fanatic. It trains our eyes and our work on this world because hope is drawn by and forward to the coming world. An apocalyptic eschatology welcomes the future because the Judge we will meet is the Redeemer. And because the Redeemer is the Creator, the future is full of promise and possibility. Because the Creator has been made flesh and is present now, we live in hope. We have hope for ourselves, for humankind—indeed, for the created order, not just Earth, but all that is, was, and shall be. The end is the triune God—Father, Son, and Holy Spirit who is determined and able to complete creation which began when God separated the light from the darkness and called it good.

JUDGMENT

For all of us must appear before the judgment seat of Christ, so that each may receive recompense for what has been done in the body, whether good or evil. —2 Cor 5:10

Some two years after its 1970 publication, I read Hal Lindsey's *The Late Great Planet Earth*. What did I know? The book scared me to death. I was not alone. The publication became the best-selling book of the 1970s. By 1990, 28 million copies were in circulation. Lindsey convinced me, if briefly, that the world was ending. Despite Jesus' warning and admission that even he did not know when the end would be, Lindsey, with slippery apology announced with a wink and a nod that he knew. The world was ending within a generation of the founding of the modern state of Israel.

Cold War warriors and their children were easy marks for Lindsey; no less so than the 68 million readers of tall tales published by Tim LaHaye and Jerry Jenkins. Their 1990s *Left Behind* series led a cottage industry of end-times profiteers. Sadly, they, and a host of other purveyors of apocalyptic

---

4. Boring, *Revelation*, 28–61.

literature, using a dark theological outlook, supported by slipshod biblical interpretation, preyed upon biblically uninformed, ill-informed, and pliable readers terrified by a world in upheaval. And they still do. The phenomenon was and is not unprecedented excepting the fortunes made by its proponents.

Dystopian escapism sells. Us-them theology sells. Appealing to dark instincts, gnawing insecurities, and socio-political disturbance, dystopian eschatology appeals to fear. It is driven by fear. It persuades by fear. And it perpetuates fear. Fear may sell books but it is morally wrong, biblically indefensible, and theologically false. Or, as Jürgen Moltmann vividly writes, "The picture of the God who judges human beings has been the cause of much spiritual and psychological damage. It has poisoned the idea of God instead of leading to trust in him. Among the dying it has intensified the fear of death through fears of hell."[5]

To counter this assault by fear, and I do not know what other name to call this theological cudgel, some Christians have so modified iterations of the God who judges in wrath as to abandon God altogether, placing instead human decision at the center. Moltmann states the revisionist narrative this way, "No one will go to heaven or be sent to hell against his will. It is a person's own decision which is followed by one or the other consequence. . . . If he believes, God will take him to heaven; if he does not believe, God will send him to hell. So doesn't this make God superfluous? Belief in the freedom of the human will replaces belief in God."[6] Said otherwise, who needs a Redeemer when a human decision will do?

Absent God, eschatology, even an apocalyptic eschatology becomes just another tired, if dangerous, version of self-help, captain-of-our-soul drivel. That said, I want to be clear about a different danger of apocalyptic eschatology. As a result of its binary outlook, apocalyptic eschatology may slip into friend-enemy thinking which neatly divides humans into sheep and goats, wheat and tares, faithful and faithless, saints and sinners. When coupled with political and military power this binary becomes extraordinarily dangerous.

Historically, eschatology, apocalyptic eschatology in particular, arose and was written from the experience and perspective of politically powerless victims. As a consequence, patience became a virtue and ultimately was made into a means of settling scores. Based on retribution which draws from a limited fund of mercy, final accounts were understood to be weighed in favor of poor and abused victims and against rich and powerful

---

5. Moltmann, *Sun of Righteousness, Arise!*, 134.
6. Moltmann, *Sun of Righteousness, Arise!*, 134.

perpetrators. Aggrieved victims appeared before the Judge as friends of God while victorious perpetrators stepped forward as enemies. And if God's enemies, why not my or our enemies? In time the victim-friend of God equivalency was transferred from the once powerless to the politically powerful and aggrieved. Armed with righteous indignation and massively destructive weapons, the aggrieved but now powerful, could, under guise of God's wrath, destroy enemies in God's name. The transfer in status from aggrieved victim to aggrieved aggressor does not square with a theology of the cross.

Jesus was crucified between two thieves. According to Luke, one derided Jesus, the other repented. Did Jesus die for one and not the other? Was he a friend to one and not the other? Moltmann makes this compelling observation which applies to friend-enemy thinking: "We do not stand before the judge on our own and dependent on ourselves, as we do here in criminal courts, or in nighttime torments of conscience. In that other judgment the perpetrators stand together with their victims, Cain with Abel, Babylon with Israel, the violent with the helpless, the murderers with the murdered, the persecutors with the martyrs.... To raise up the oppressed is one side of the truth; to make the blind see is the other side."[7] The prophet Isaiah made a like declaration in images, "The wolf shall live with the lamb, the leopard shall lie down with the kid, the calf and the lion and the fatling together . . . for the earth will be full of the knowledge of the LORD as the waters cover the sea" (Isa 11:6–9). Knowledge of God alters everything, including friend-enemy thinking.

We will appear before the Judge to give an account. But victims and perpetrators and silent watchers alike will stand shoulder to shoulder as among thieves when they appear before Christ. Christ does not first punish; Christ reconciles. Christ does not first reward; he mends the broken, transforms the distorted, and releases the captive. As a consequence of God's judgment, perpetrators are no longer predators and victims are no longer prey. Roles are not simply reversed. They are uprooted, destroyed, and remade. Judgment brings peace to victims and perpetrators. Or, as Jesus says, "Peace I leave with you; my peace I give to you. I do not give to you *as the world gives*" (John 14:27). Christ separates the righteous from the wicked in order to reconcile the righteous and the wicked. In Christ, justice and mercy meet for victims and perpetrators and silent watchers alike. God's judgment in Christ completes creation.

---

7. Moltmann, *Sun of Righteousness, Arise!*, 139.

NEW CREATION

Then I saw a new heaven and a new earth; for the first heaven and the first earth had passed away, and the sea was no more. —Rev 21:1

One day I will die. One day you will die. One day Earth itself will cease to exist. Theology and science agree on these three. But will we live again? Will there be a new heaven and a new earth, a new you and me? Faith answers *yes*.

In answering yes, the Bible ignites imagination using multiple symbols: a heavenly city, a father's house, a marriage feast, paradise, and, among others symbols, the peaceable kingdom pictured by Isaiah. No symbol, perhaps, is more evocative and expansive than the new heaven and new earth of John's Apocalypse, where "the sea was no more."

Christian theology employs multiple signs to talk about life after death such as resurrection of the body, immortality, eternal life, and life everlasting. In keeping with what I have termed an apocalyptic eschatology, I would make the following observations.

Signs and symbols reference some-thing, the former directly, the latter indirectly. As Feinberg and Mallatt observe, "the adaptive importance of sensory consciousness is that natural selection has sustained it over the past half-billion years by making the vertebrates' subjective image and affects match reality closely, or at least as closely as needed for survival."[8] Signs and symbols, regardless of their origin, are abstractions but both have referents. While signs point to their referent, symbols hint at theirs. So how do we know that signs and symbols refer to some-thing that is true or real and not some-thing that is false or imagined? Science and theology must each reckon with falsification and verification. Both must also reckon with abstractions which push against the barriers of imagination and reason. Can you imagine the universe squeezed to the size of a single atom? Sounds fantastical, doesn't it? But that is what the Big Bang invites us to consider. That doesn't mean the theory is false or imagined, but it does push against rational capacity and imagination.

Signs and symbols reference ultimate realities by pushing against the limitations of reason and imagination. The introduction to this chapter walked through eight billion years in three hundred or so words. Given the life expectancy of Earth what do words like day or hour or year or century or millennium mean? We use these signs to talk about near things, seemingly manageable things like getting married before we are thirty or having kids

---

8. Feinberg and Mallett, *The Ancient Origins of Consciousness*, 219.

by thirty-five or retiring when we are seventy or when referencing the millennia of ancient or future history; but what do these time signatures mean in the context of planetary time measured not in thousand-year increments but million-plus-year increments? When located in a non-anthropocentric timeframe, humans are incredibly short-lived and reduced to near insignificance, which recalls the psalmist, "When I look at your heavens, the work of your fingers, the moon and the stars that you have established; what are human beings that you are mindful of them, mortals that you care for them" (Ps 8:3–4).

When speaking about new creation, eternal life, and resurrection of the body, we bump up against the limits of language, but bump we must. That does not make us foolish or wrong but frees us to imagine the life God desires and is making for us all. With these limitations in mind, I invite you to consider one sign and three symbols: resurrection of the body, paradise, the sea that was no more, and a new heaven and a new earth.

Resurrection of the body means that who we are in this life is not lost in the next. It means that eternal life is God's gracious gift, a work of new creation and not an extension of this life or a continuation of an imagined immortal part of us. Humans are embodied souls or in-souled bodies. We are not one or the other but both together. God does not raise an idea of you; God raises you from the dead. The disciples recognized the risen Lord which means that in the life to come we will recognize one another. Recognition means that identity is not lost. It also means that identity is not simply continued, it is transformed—"we will be like him" (1 John 3:3). Or, as Paul puts it, "Just as we have borne the image of the man of dust, we will also bear the image of the man of heaven . . . we will all be changed, in a moment, in the twinkling of an eye . . . (1 Cor 15:49–52).

Scripture is silent about many details of heaven. One exception—there is no marriage (Matt 22:30), suggesting that resurrected identity is not first defined by designations like wife or husband, mother or father, sister or brother, etc. Of greater importance, as Paul writes, "we will see [God] face to face." Moreover, "[n]ow I know only in part," he says of this world, "then I will know fully," he says of the next, "even as I have been fully known" here and now (1 Cor 13:12). Resurrection of the body means that we will see God and know one another.

When Jesus was crucified he told the thief on the cross, "Truly I tell you, today you will be with me in paradise" (Luke 23:43). Anticipating the outcome of his imprisonment, coupled with his desire to continue his proclamation of the gospel, Paul could say, "I am hard pressed between the two: my desire is to depart and be with Christ, for that is far better; but to remain in the flesh is more necessary for you" (Phil 1:23–24). Both texts support a conviction that when we die we will immediately see God. Luke's word *paradise* refers to a cultivated garden, a park of sorts. As we will see, other references associate heaven with a heavenly city or new Jerusalem—so maybe a park within a city? I am teasing, in part anyway. The greater message is immediacy. When we die we will see God, straight away, without delay. We will enter paradise.

Planetary science tells us that Earth will lose its oceans, completely lose them, two billion years from now. John imagined the death of a different sea—one which is the reservoir of evil and home to the red dragon, the sea which will be no more when the first heaven and the first earth pass away (Rev 13, 20). Or, as Paul wrote to the Corinthians, "The last enemy to be destroyed is death" (1 Cor 15:26). Jesus is more than a King of Hearts. In the apocalyptic eschatology of the New Testament, Jesus destroys the powers of sin, evil, suffering, and death. "He will wipe every tear from their eyes. Death will be no more; mourning and crying and pain will be no more, for the first things have passed away" (Rev 21:4). Or, again, as it is written in Isaiah, "As a mother comforts her child, so I will comfort you" (Isa 66: 13). John's sea that was no more represents God's victory over evil. In John's vision, hell itself will be no more. It will be cast into the lake of fire and annihilated (Rev 20:14). In that day when God is "all in all" (1 Cor 15:28), hell will not exist. Temporal sins do not bear the weight of eternal torment. God will not permit it.

Few images of Christian hope surpass John's symbol of "a new heaven and a new earth." This look around began with an iteration of our 13.8 billion-year-old universe. It ends with billions upon billions of years to come, among them, Earth's physical annihilation 7.9 billion years from now. What does John's new earth have to do with that Earth? Calvin was wise to caution against venturing into unknowns by attempting to say more than we can know. I do not know how John's symbol intersects with planetary science any more than I know *how* God raises the dead. I only know if God can squeeze the known mass and space-time universe into an atom-sized point of singularity, God can make a new heaven and a new earth. And I know that only because I believe the Redeemer lives.

HOPE

Then comes the end, when he hands over the kingdom to God the Father, after he has destroyed every ruler and authority and power. For he must reign until he has put all his enemies under his feet. The last enemy to be destroyed is death. . . . When all things are subjected to him, then the Son himself will also be subjected to the one who put all things in subjection under him, so that God may be all in all. —1 Cor 15:24–28

Nicholas Christakis, whom we met in the previous chapter, observes that "evolution does not know where it is going. It has no overarching objective, no endgame. . . . Genes are just a way that biological systems store and transmit information."[9] I admire the professor's honesty, scientific acumen, but most of all his modesty. His standards merit imitation. This chapter will achieve some measure of those standards if it helps readers live with hope because of the One to whom we are going. The triune God is the end. The triune God is our destination and consequentially also our way, our truth, and our life (John 14:6). This hope does not allow us to disappear or retreat or withdraw from responsibility for the world. Faith does not absolve us of responsibility for the ways we arrange social power or how we each live personally. Faith brings these and other responsibilities into sharp relief guiding us to God's will. We are stewards and shepherds of Earth, not owners or masters, but servants of the gifts entrusted to us. Life is best lived when we move from an anthropocentric mode of being in the world to a theocentric mode of being. That way of being in the world is the pathway of hope led by Jesus Christ the crucified who is risen and alive among all people.

Hope is the end of nihilism, the most lethal and pervasive threat to human life today. The threat of nihilism is greater than the ecological crisis, greater than the prospect of nuclear war or techno-amusement or sociopolitical revolution. Nihilism is the demonic force beneath these and other threats. Hope is not just an idea; it is a power which resists and overcomes all threats to human life. Hope has the power to move us from being amused spectators to critically thinking participants. Hope moves us from being aggrieved victims and aggressive victors to compassionate conquerors ruled by the Prince of Peace. Hope moves us from the "closed circle of our humanity" to live in the presence of the Holy One. Hope remakes the soul. Hope not only opens our eyes to our complicity in evil but also stands us on our feet freeing us to walk in justice and mercy. God did not create us to grovel but to walk upright, shoulder to shoulder, and side by side in communion with fellow humans. Hope yields neither to whining pessimism nor crowing optimism. Hope endures because it is fueled by the passionate fire of God who does not rest or grow weary until Sabbath dawns.

---

9. Christakis, *Blueprint*, 183.

Sabbath does not take us back to the beginning but moves us forward to the end. The end is Christ, who, when he has "destroyed every ruler and authority and power," will hand over the kingdom to God the Father "so that God may be all in all." This march toward Sabbath began on the first day when God "separated the light from the darkness." Sabbath broke into our day when on the third day Christ was raised from the dead and was known in the breaking of bread to disciples with hearts disbelieving and wondering with joy (Luke 24:28-35). Sabbath will be complete in that day when the city will have no temple "for its temple is the Lord." On that day, the city will have no "need of sun or moon to shine on it, for the glory of God is its light, and its lamp is the Lamb. The nations will walk by its light . . ." (Rev 21:22-24). Our end, as our beginning, is God who called the light out of the darkness creating life.

Chapter 21

Where Are You?

FLYING THROUGH THE UNIVERSE

But the LORD God called to the man, and said to him, "Where are you?" —Gen 3:9

Where are you? According to my phone GPS as I write this, I am roughly thirty-one degrees north and eighty-eight degrees west or approximately 1,850 miles north of the equator and 5,300 miles west of the Prime Meridian. If those coordinates don't ring a bell, would it help if I said I was 587 miles southeast of Wiseman's View or a nine-hour, seven-minute drive from that scenic overlook in Pisgah National Forest, pending traffic, road conditions, and stops? Still not oriented? How about if I said I was 93 million miles from the sun, riding along among several hundred billion stars that make up our galaxy, and that our solar system, traveling at over 500,000 miles per hour, was in the Perseus arm of the Milky Way about halfway from the center of our galaxy? Would it help if I noted that our beautifully named but humble-sized galaxy with *only* 250 billion stars was one of thirty or so galaxies traveling among an estimated 100 billion galaxies in the observable universe? Still not sure where I am? What if I said in was in Mobile, Alabama? Mobile is about twenty-seven miles northeast of Bayou La Batre, Alabama, or about halfway between New Orleans, Louisiana, and Panama City, Florida. Does that help?

Location is determined by relationship—one position related to another—which is handy when looking around. One position relative to another, like our solar system relative to our galaxy, may provide some measure of orientation within our vast star-jammed universe. But where exactly is the universe? Since we do not have a referent outside of the universe, we cannot actually say *where* the universe is—it just is. If infinite, the universe has no center or edge which means that one set of coordinates within the universe is just as much the center as any other set—so wherever we are is the center. And that means that every other entity in the universe, like us or way unlike us, is also at the center. These observations, contradictory sounding though they are, may help when looking around this life. But I digress, but only slightly.

Where are you? It was a strange question for a deity to ask. But so the Bible says God asked Adam. On second thought, you may have been asked something like that by a parent, say, your mother. When she asked where you had been she already knew by the red mud on your shoes. She knew that you had been where you shouldn't have been because she had warned you multiple times that there were water moccasins down by the creek at the foot of the red dirt hill. The real question was *did we know?* When she asked where we had been, she was not asking about our itinerary. She was asking about our listening not because she was worried about water moccasins but because we needed to be worried, cautious—the backyard could be dangerous. Her question was not driven by a quest for our whereabouts. Her interest was freighted with care, her unconquerable, inseparable love for us, which she put at risk when we went out to play.

Where are you? Adam doesn't answer, *Oh, I've been down by the creek, just hanging around.* Adam says, "I heard the sound of you in the garden, and I was afraid, because I was naked; and I hid myself" (Gen 3:10).

The *where* of Adam is defined by his proximity to God who was close enough to be heard walking. The *where* of Adam is defined by fear which crawled into his throat when he heard footsteps. Why fear? Why not indifference or playfulness like when you told your mother, *Oh, I was just fooling around.* Why fear? Does Adam know something about God that we don't know? Is he privy to insider information? The only clue given by the narrative is the warning. After permitting Adam to "freely eat of every tree," God warns Adam not to eat "of the tree of the knowledge of good and evil . . . for in the day that you eat of it *you shall die.*" Does Adam conclude from this warning that God is fearful and dreadful or that fearful and dreadful consequences may come if a limit is transgressed?

Where does Adam get the idea that he should "be afraid" when he hears footsteps in the garden? Was God scowling when he issued the warning? Did God speak sharply? Was there something in the tone of God's voice? Whence Adam's fear when he heard footsteps? Did fear come from his knowledge of God's character? And was that God's intent when he issued the warning—to make Adam afraid, very afraid lest he step out of line? A clue is given when Adam answers, "I heard the sound of you in the garden, and I was afraid, because I was naked; and I hid myself."

"I was afraid, because I was naked." Not, I was afraid when I heard the sound of you. Adam's nakedness, like the red dirt on our shoes, is the culprit, not God's fierce love. God immediately suspects a changed circumstance, "Have you eaten from the tree of which I commanded you not to eat?" Prior to eating the forbidden fruit there was no shame. The forbidden fruit does not create distance, estrangement, and dis-location. The narrative does not attribute magical power to the fruit, but rather ascribes dis-location and hence shame and fear to a breach of trust. The breach of trust creates dis-location allowing the intrusion of fear and shame. What are we to make of fear and shame? Do they indicate location? Might naked and afraid define where we are?

No matter how far or near we look around, whether we look closely and personally or take a far-off, impersonal look into deep space, we sense something of what this strange but familiar story is talking about—we feel naked and afraid. Nakedness includes shame but vulnerability comes closer to the experience. And leave God out of the picture, not that you would. But for purposes of this thought experiment, exclude God. Assume there is no God. God does not exist. Who are you? What are you? And where are you going as you fly through an infinite universe? Answer those questions. And if the answers don't make you afraid, I don't know what to say. Having even a fractional awareness of our location is enough to make us fearful. Awareness of our location in the vastness of the universe is fascinating, exhilarating, enchanting, and all the rest—but if not also fearful and vulnerable, then I would check my honesty if not my pulse.

With that said, naked and afraid is not sufficient for faith. We have not truly experienced naked and afraid until we have come into close proximity of the living God. Faith is determined by its subject. And the Subject of faith is not fearsome as in our worst nightmare, but fearsome because God fiercely loves his creation. To be truly naked and afraid is to realize that we are created from love for love to love. And that the creating and redeeming Lover is most fully and completely disclosed on a cross between thieves on a rocky hill beyond the city.[1] The African American spiritual, "Were You There?,"

---

1. Moltmann, *The Crucified God*, 40.

better expresses what I am struggling to say, "Sometimes it causes me to tremble, tremble, tremble. Were you there when they crucified my Lord?"[2]

God desires neither our fear nor our shame. "Fear not" is the typical rejoinder when God appears in the Bible. "The fear of the LORD is the beginning of wisdom" (Prov 9:10), but that kind of fear is best described as the kind which makes us remove our shoes because we are walking on holy ground. Fear of the Lord reveals the holiness of God which Genesis represents with reference to shame. Bonhoeffer distinguished guilt from shame saying that "shame is more original than remorse. The peculiar fact that we lower our eyes when a stranger's eye meets our gaze is not a sign of remorse for a fault, but a sign of that shame which, when it knows that it is seen, is reminded of something that it lacks, namely, the lost wholeness of life, its own nakedness."[3] Neither shame nor guilt is commensurate with the rule of God's love; not because we are guiltless or shame-free, but because God's holy love newly makes us. We become children of God not by an accident of birth but by hearing the footsteps that cause our hearts to fear, rustlings made by the Creator who comes as our Redeemer bidding us, "Do not be afraid; I am the first and the last, and the living one. . ." (Rev 1:17).

RETURN TO PISGAH

Then Moses went up from the plains of Moab to Mount Nebo, to the top of Pisgah, which is opposite Jericho, and the LORD showed him the whole land. . . . The LORD said to him . . . "I have let you see it with your own eyes, But you shall not cross over there." Then Moses, the servant of the LORD, died there in the land of Moab, at the LORD's command. —Deut 43:1, 4–5

Moses' death on Pisgah is inexplicable and tragic.[4] It is also ironic, an irony exaggerated by the burial of Moses in an unmarked, undisclosed location. The irony is painfully enforced by the fact that God led Moses up the mountain and "showed" him the land he could not enter, despite the fact that Moses had led God's people for forty years beginning in Egypt. Moses' death on Pisgah is evidence of the tragic consequence of sin and the strange consolation of grace.

---

2. Presbyterian Church (U.S.A.), *Glory to God*, hymn no. 228.
3. Bonhoeffer, *Ethics*, 20.
4. Miller, *Deuteronomy*, 243.

The impending death of Moses is mentioned multiple times in Deuteronomy. Each mention alludes to his non-entry into the land or non-inheritance of the promise made to Abraham. Two texts explicitly state that Moses may not enter because God was angry at Moses "on account of the people" (Deut 1:37, 3:26). A third says that Moses was denied because he along with Aaron "broke faith" with God at Meribath-kadesh where Israel "quarreled and tested" God (Deut 32:51). While these explanations likely come from different hands, accounting for differing reasons cited for exclusion, the biting sting of exclusion is by no means dissipated. Moses suffers the consequences of sin, whether his own or his people's or some combination of the two. Despite this, or perhaps because of it, the testament to Moses ends with high praise for Israel's greatest prophet and wonder worker whom God knew "face to face" as no other (Deut 34:10).

Though streaked by dawning grace, the view from Pisgah remains clouded by sin, which is worth remembering while walking in the twenty-first century. Being saved, found, born again, chosen, awake, or whatever other descriptor used to denote Christian discipleship, does not make twenty-first-century sojourners immune to spiritual pride and moral arrogance. Grace makes us more fully aware that glory belongs to God and not to us, which should make us humbly proud, not proudly humble.

Moses' death on Pisgah reminds us that we stand as sinners among sinners, not sinless and above sinners. While the New Testament does not specifically mention Pisgah, the writer of Hebrews, recalling Israel's wilderness sojourn, reminded his readers that they should "take care" so that "none may have an evil, unbelieving heart that turns away from the living God. [E]xhort one another every day," he writes, ". . . so that none of you may be hardened by the deceitfulness of sin. For we have become partners of Christ, if only we hold our first confidence firm to the end" (Heb 3:12–14).

Perseverance, unlike presumptive arrogance and smug self-righteousness, enables followers to stand firm in their convictions, but only by holding fast to Christ. Standing with Moses on Pisgah puts us in good company for looking around in the twenty-first century when so many are watching and waiting for signs of hope from credible witnesses. Credible witnesses do not stand apart from, but rather with, fellow sinners as they bear witness to the Creator who is redeeming creation by making all things new. The horizon of this hope is made more, not less, credible when people of faith testify to the strange consolation of grace which teaches hearts to fear and makes them humbly proud to be called children of God.

THE PRODIGAL FATHER

Then Jesus said, "There was a man who had two sons...." —Luke 15:1

This look around began with the story of Cain and Abel; it draws to a close with a story of two other brothers (Luke 15:11–32). Neither is formally named. Each is known only by his age—the younger who received his inheritance in advance and goes to a far country and the elder who remains dutifully behind. As with the former story, so the latter has a third actor. And, as in the first story, this other is known by his speech and acts. He is named, quite simply, *father*.

In view of the younger who squanders his inheritance in lavish and dissolute living, Bibles and Bible interpreters routinely label this passage the parable of the Prodigal Son. The parable is more aptly titled the Prodigal Father.

Stories and parables are classic because they surface and cast piercing light on recurring themes played on a large human stage. This one is no different. We hear this story and wonder about ourselves, those we love, and some we don't even know. Perhaps like the younger you have wandered into the far country or maybe you are thinking about it or you are halfway there. Or maybe like the younger you are deep into the far country and can't get back. Returning is not your first thought or your last. It has not occurred to you, crossed your mind. You have not given it a second thought because now flush with cash and carefree you need not be care-full. You have no worries. It is not that you are indifferent. You make expected phone calls and the annual pilgrimage home. And maybe the old pastor calls you by name though you have forgotten hers. Or maybe the new guy greeting at the door is otherwise occupied when you pass by and it is just as well—you are another face in the crowd—so what?

Or maybe you have stopped calling. Who knows why that happens—sharp words exchanged over a wine-laced Thanksgiving opened old wounds or new ones were freshly made when you announced your political persuasion or introduced a new family member less than warmly received? Maybe you just don't care to go home—maybe because you were never home. You did not fit in then and you sure as hell don't fit now. Why must you always accommodate, acquiesce, or pretend you still believe when hands join and prayer begins, *Heavenly, Father, we thank thee for these and all our many blessings*. What bull. Your old man was always on the job, and whenever he was home he complained about work and how unfairly he was paid. Thankful? Hardly. And your poor mother.... So far as you were concerned she got saint of the year for putting up with the old man. Seeing her now, tired and half herself, is just too sad—you stay away buried in work or the latest distraction.

Or maybe you have been wondering—is there something there? Could it be true? Is there something you have missed that you cannot name but imagine possible. You are intrigued but remain resolute in your assessment. Faith is . . . well . . . vain, childish, infantile, magic-laced wishful thinking. God talk—that's all it is—talk. But you lie awake at night unable to dodge arresting thoughts, *plagued* may be the better word, especially when daydreaming of what might be if the talk was not just—talk. What if it is true?

Or maybe you have made a turn toward home. You have inquired through friends, dabbled in freshman philosophy and spent more than one late night over beers contending with large notions about emergent properties or laughed or winced or laughingly winced about the weird co-worker who puts ants on you when he talks about Jeezus. And don't mention the whack-a-doddles on TV with greasy palms and greasier smiles. What a joke. But once you stumbled sleepy-eyed, if slightly hung-over, into an eleven o'clock service. And it was not half-bad. The place smelled ancient or maybe it was just *Old Spice* drifting from the old guy in the next pew. You thought about going back, but convinced yourself the rough patch would pass and soon enough it did. Still, now that it has yielded, you find yourself wondering—*Could it be true?*

Or maybe like the younger you returned. At the time, it seemed like a good idea. And it has been good for you. The far country was no picnic and you would have given anything back then to be where you are now. It felt so right—this shiny new thing called faith. Your old world was upended, suspended. You had to leave it behind and you did. You started over—a brand new page, a new and better you. And people noticed. How could they not? You seemed more confident, grounded, happy even, as in happy-for-the-first-time happy. Not rock concert happy that vanishes when the ringing in your ears stops. This happiness was the real deal, authentic. When you were greeted by extravagant love and everybody at your party was having a good time, you never felt better.

Tick-tock. Years have passed from that distant time and now you understand why your elder brother refused to join your party. Now you are with him. If you didn't get his steely edge when you first returned, you do now. You have been to one too many team meetings, strategy sessions, and Bible studies. You have heard one too many sermons about the same old stuff. You have had your fill of fundraising and sacrificial giving and walking the straight and narrow. Not that you would get off the path but you sure hate being there. You see you walking through the door and mutter loudly in your mind so that no one hears—*what a fool, another sucker for*

God, but you dare not say out loud what screams inside your head. You are now stuck, stuck with your elder brother—insider out. I believe, help my unbelief. You want to believe but even that prayer floats no higher than the bedroom ceiling.

"While [the younger] was still far off, his father saw him and was filled with compassion; he ran and put his arms around him and kissed him. . . . The father said to [the elder], 'Son you are always with me, and all that is mine is yours.'" Who is this Prodigal Father who leaves dignity behind, flouting wisdom and convention by his daring, overwhelming love for the younger? Who is this Prodigal Father who in the same love leaves the party to plead with the elder—"Come celebrate. This brother of yours was dead and has come to life; he was lost and has been found." And why do father problems always also become brother problems? "Am I my brother's keeper?" Or why are brother problems ultimately also father problems? "Cain was very angry, and his countenance fell." Are we happy for a sister or brother only to the extent that we are happy with our Father? And if so, why does the Father keep returning us to our sisters and brothers?

Who is this Prodigal Father, the Ancient of Days, the one who was dead but is now alive and bids us, *Come and see. Abide with me. Follow me. I no longer call you servants, for I have called you friends. No one has greater love than this, to lay down one's life for one's friends. You are my friends if you do what I command you—love one another as I have loved you. I am with you always.*

Walking in this age, as in any and every age, is like walking on the edge of a very high cliff or flying through the universe, take your pick. The One who bids us to come and follow, the same who welcomes us home, also goes before us—Jesus the author and perfector of our faith. Even now wherever we are he cries aloud and whispers, *Come, follow me.*

Bibliography

Anwar, Yasmin. "New study debunks myth of Cahokia's Native American lost civilization." *Science Daily*, January 27, 2020. https://www.sciencedaily.com/releases/2020/01/200127145457.htm.

Barth, Karl. *Church Dogmatics*. Vol. 3.3, *The Doctrine of Creation*. Translated by G. W. Bromiley and R. J. Ehrlich. Edinburgh: T. & T. Clark, 1960.

———. *The Epistle to the Romans*. Translated by Edwyn C. Hoskins. New York: Oxford University Press, 1977.

Bellah, Robert N. *Religion in Human Evolution: From the Paleolithic to the Axial Age*. Cambridge, MA: Harvard University Press, 2011.

Bethge, Eberhard. *Dietrich Bonhoeffer: Man of Vision—Man of Courage*. Translated by Eric Mosbacher et al. New York: Harper & Row, 1970.

Bonhoeffer, Dietrich. *The Cost of Discipleship*. 1st Touchstone ed. Translated by R. H. Fuller. New York: Touchstone, 1995.

———. *Ethics*. Edited by Eberhard Bethge. Translated by Neville Horton Smith. New York: Macmillan, 1955.

———. *Letters & Papers From Prison*. Translated by Reginald Fuller et al. New York: Macmillan, 1972.

Boring, M. Eugene. *Revelation*. Interpretation: A Bible Commentary for Teaching and Preaching. Louisville: Westminster John Knox, 1989.

Brueggemann, Walter. *Genesis*. Interpretation: A Bible Commentary for Teaching and Preaching. Atlanta: John Knox, 1982.

Brueggemann, Walter, et al. *General and Old Testament Articles, Genesis, Exodus, Leviticus*. New Interpreter's Bible 1. Nashville: Abingdon, 1994.

Calvin, John. *Institutes of the Christian Religion*. Edited by John T. McNeill. Translated by Ford Lewis Battles. Library of Christian Classics. Philadelphia: Westminster, 1960.

Carter, Stephen L. *The Culture of Disbelief: How American Law and Politics Trivialize Religious Devotion*. New York: Basic, 1993.

Christakis, Nicholas A. *Blueprint: The Evolutionary Origins Of A Good Society*. New York: Little, Brown Spark, 2019.

Christian, David. *Origin Story: A Big History of Everything*. New York: Little, Brown Spark, 2018.

Congressional Medal of Honor Society. "Halyburton, William David, Jr." www.cmohsorg/recipient-detail/2771/halyburton-william-david-jr.php.

Diamond, Jared. *Collapse: How Societies Choose to Fail or Succeed*. Civilizations Rise and Fall 2. New York: Viking, 2005.

———. *Guns, Germs, And Steel: The Fates of Human Societies*. Civilizations Rise and Fall 1. New York: Norton, 2005.

———. *Upheaval: Turning Points for Nations In Crisis*. Civilizations Rise and Fall 3. New York: Little, Brown and Company, 2019.

Dunn, James D. G. *Romans 1-8*. Word Biblical Commentary 38A. Dallas: Thomas Nelson, 1988.

Feinberg, Todd E., and Jon M. Mallatt. *The Ancient Origins of Consciousness: How the Brain Created Experience*. Cambridge, MA: MIT Press, 2016.

Fuller, Robert C. *Spiritual but not Religious: Understanding Unchurched America*. New York: Oxford University Press, 2001.

Gallup. "Religion." In Depth: Topics A to Z. https//news.gallup.com/poll/1690/religion.aspx.

Greenway, William N. A. "Cosmodicy: On Evil and the Problem with Theodicy." *Insights: The Faculty Journal of Austin Seminary* (Spring 2006) 36–40. https://www.austinseminary.edu/uploaded/about_us/pdf/insights/insights_spring_06.pdf.

Guthrie Jr., Shirley C. *Christian Doctrine*. Rev. ed. Louisville: Westminster John Knox, 1994.

Haidt, Jonathan. *The Righteous Mind: Why Good People Are Divided By Politics and Religion*. New York: Vintage, 2013.

Harari, Yuval Noah. *Sapiens: A Brief History of Humankind*. New York: HarperCollins, 2015.

Heine, Steven J. *DNA is Not Destiny: The Remarkable, Completely Misunderstood Relationship between You and Your Genes*. New York: Norton, 2017.

Johnson, Dominic. *God Is Watching You: How the Fear of God Makes Us Human*. New York: Oxford University Press, 2016.

Kierkegaard, Søren. *Concluding Unscientific Postscript*. Translated by David F. Swenson and Walter Lowrie. Princeton, NJ: Princeton University Press, 1941.

Kuhn, Thomas S. *The Structure of Scientific Revolutions*. 2nd ed. Chicago: University of Chicago Press, 1970.

Latour, Bruno. *Down to Earth: Politics in the New Climate Regime*. Translated by Catherine Porter. Medford, MA: Polity, 2018.

Lewis, Simon L., and Mark A. Maslin. *The Human Planet: How We Created The Anthropocene*. New Haven, CT: Yale University Press, 2018.

Lindbeck, George A. *The Nature of Doctrine: Religion and Theology in a Postliberal Age*. 25th anniversary ed. Louisville: Westminster John Knox, 2009.

Migliore, Daniel L. *Faith Seeking Understanding: An Introduction to Christian Theology*. Grand Rapids: Eerdmans, 1991.

Miller, Patrick. *Deuteronomy*. Interpretation: A Bible Commentary for Teaching and Preaching. Louisville: Westminster John Knox, 1990.

Moltmann, Jürgen. *The Church in the Power of the Spirit: A Contribution to Messianic Ecclesiology*. Translated by Margaret Kohl. New York: Harper & Row, 1977.

———. *The Crucified God: The Cross of Christ as the Foundation and Criticism of Christian Theology*. Translated by R. A. Wilson and John Bowden. New York: Harper & Row, 1974.

———. *God in Creation: A New Theology of Creation and the Spirit of God*. Translated by Margaret Kohl. San Francisco: HarperSanFrancisco, 1985.

———. *Sun of Righteousness, Arise!: God's Future for Humanity and the Earth*. Translated by Margaret Kohl. Minneapolis: Fortress, 2010.

———. *Theology of Hope: On the Ground and the Implications of Christian Eschatology*. Translated by James W. Leitch. New York: Harper & Row, 1965.

———. *The Way of Jesus Christ: Christology in Messianic Dimensions*. Translated by Margaret Kohl. New York: HarperCollins, 1990.

Morse, Christopher. *Not Every Spirit: A Dogmatics of Christian Disbelief*. 2nd ed. London: T. & T. Clark, 2009.

NASA. "Continents in Collision: Pangea Ultima." NASA Science. October 5, 2000. https://science.nasa.gov/science-news/science-at-nasa/2000/ast06oct_1.

Nebelsick, Harold. *Theology and Science in Mutual Modification*. New York: Oxford University Press, 1981.

Pew Research Center. "How Americans view their jobs." Social & Demographic Trends. http//www.pewsocialtrends.org/2016/10/06/3.

Pinker, Steven. *The Better Angels of Our Nature: Why Violence Has Declined*. New York: Penguin, 2011.

Polanyi, Michael. *Personal Knowledge: Towards a Post-Critical Philosophy*. Chicago: University of Chicago Press, 1958.

Postman, Neil. *Amusing Ourselves to Death: Public Discourse in the Age of Show Business*. 20th anniversary ed. New York: Penguin, 2005.

Presbyterian Church (U.S.A.). *Book of Common Worship, Pastoral Edition*. Louisville: Westminster John Knox, 1993.

———. *The Constitution of the Presbyterian Church (U.S.A.): Part I, Book of Confessions*. Louisville: Office of the General Assembly, 1996.

———. *The Constitution of the Presbyterian Church (U.S.A.): Part II, Book of Order 2015–2017*. Louisville: Office of the General Assembly, 2015.

———. *Glory to God: The Presbyterian Hymnal*. Louisville: Westminster John Knox, 2013.

Rahman, Shameema. "Frequent Reference Question: How Many Federal Laws Are There?" Library of Congress. *In Custodia Legis: Law Librarians of Congress*, March 12, 2013. https://blogs.loc.gov/law/2013/03/frequent-reference-question-how-many-federal-laws-are-there/.

Ritchie, Hannah, and Max Roser. "Causes of Death." Our World in Data. Last modified December 2019. https://ourworldindata.org/causes-of-death.

Rutledge, Fleming. *The Crucifixion: Understanding the Death of Jesus Christ*. Grand Rapids: Eerdmans, 2015.

Stark, Rodney. *The Rise of Christianity: How the Obscure, Marginal Jesus Movement Became the Dominant Religious Force in the Western World in a Few Centuries*. San Francisco: HarperSanFrancisco, 1997.

Volf, Miroslav. *Free of Charge: Giving and Forgiving in a Culture Stripped of Grace*. Grand Rapids: Zondervan, 2005.

Wathey, John C. *The Illusion of God's Presence: The Biological Origins of Spiritual Longing*. Amherst, NY: Prometheus, 2016.

Wikipedia. "Justice as Fairness." Last modified February 12, 2020. https://en.wikipedia.org/wiki/Justice_as_Fairness.

———. "List of Christian denominations by number of members." Last modified May 17, 2020. https://en.wikipedia.org/wiki/List_of_Christian_denominations_by_number_of_members.

———. "Timeline of the far future." Last modified May 21, 2020. https://en.wikipedia.org/wiki/Timeline_of_the_far_future.

World Council of Churches. "Baptism, Eucharist and Ministry: Faith and Order paper no. 111, the 'Lima Text.'" World Council of Churches meeting, Geneva, Switzerland, January 15, 1982. https://www.oikoumene.org/en/resources/documents/commissions/faith-and-order/i-unity-the-church-and-its-mission/baptism-eucharist-and-ministry-faith-and-order-paper-no-111-the-lima-text.

www.ingramcontent.com/pod-product-compliance
Lightning Source LLC
Chambersburg PA
CBHW051930160426
43198CB00012B/2098